AF262887

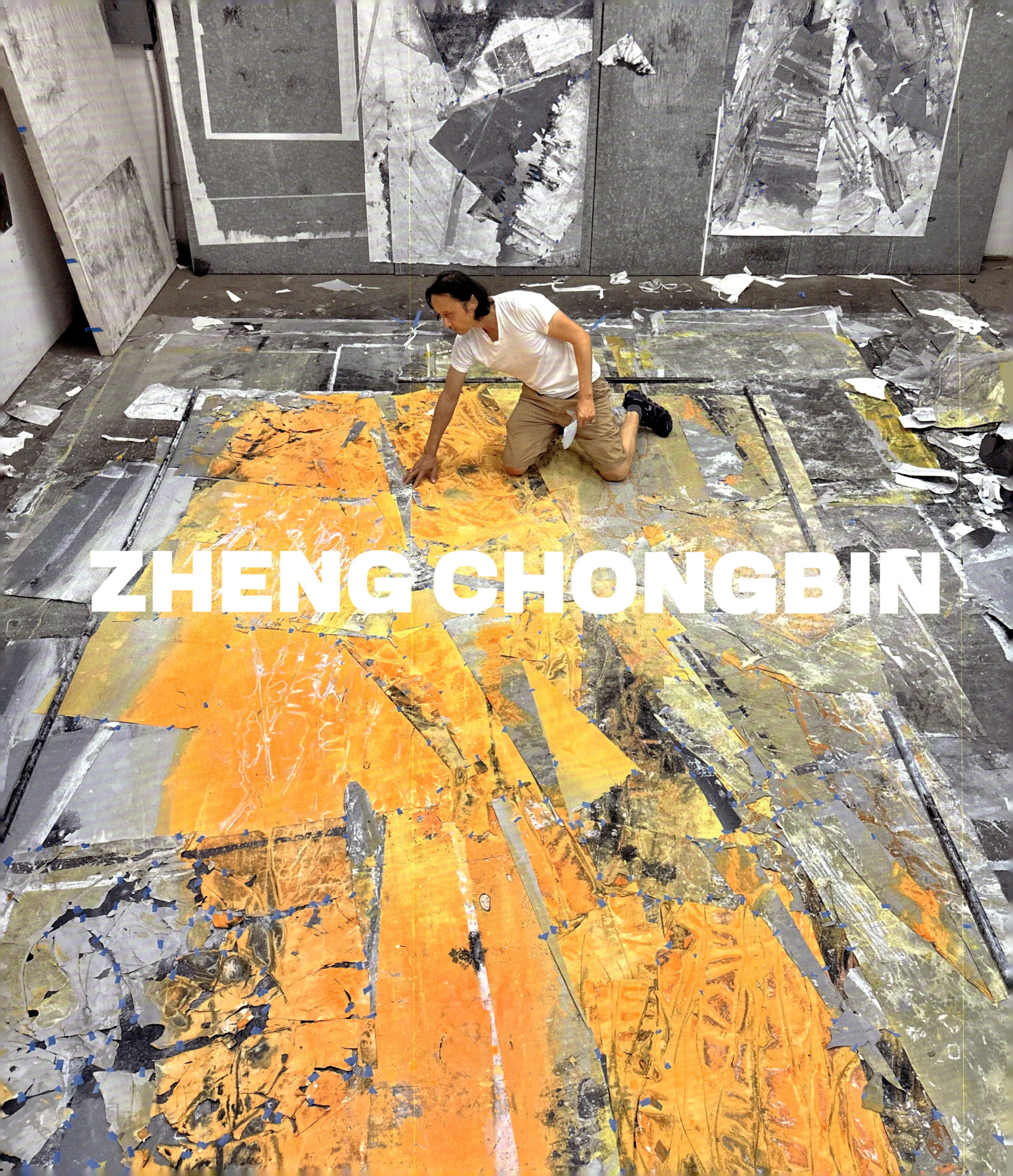

ZHENG CHONGBIN

GOLDEN STATE

Susanna Ferrell
Michael Govan
Celia Yang

Edited by **Susanna Ferrell**

INK Institute
in association with
Los Angeles County Museum of Art

DelMonico Books · D.A.P.
New York

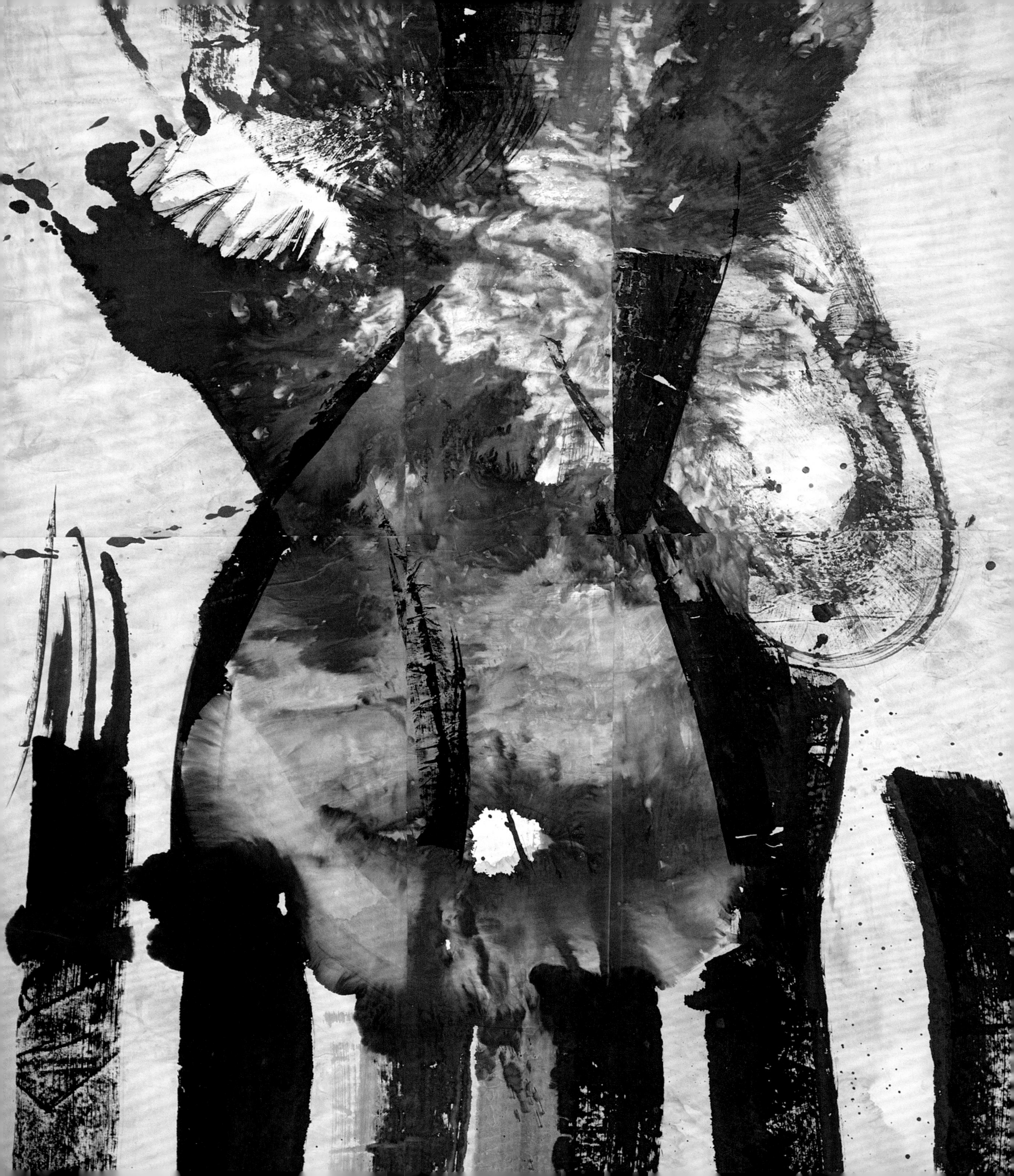

Contents

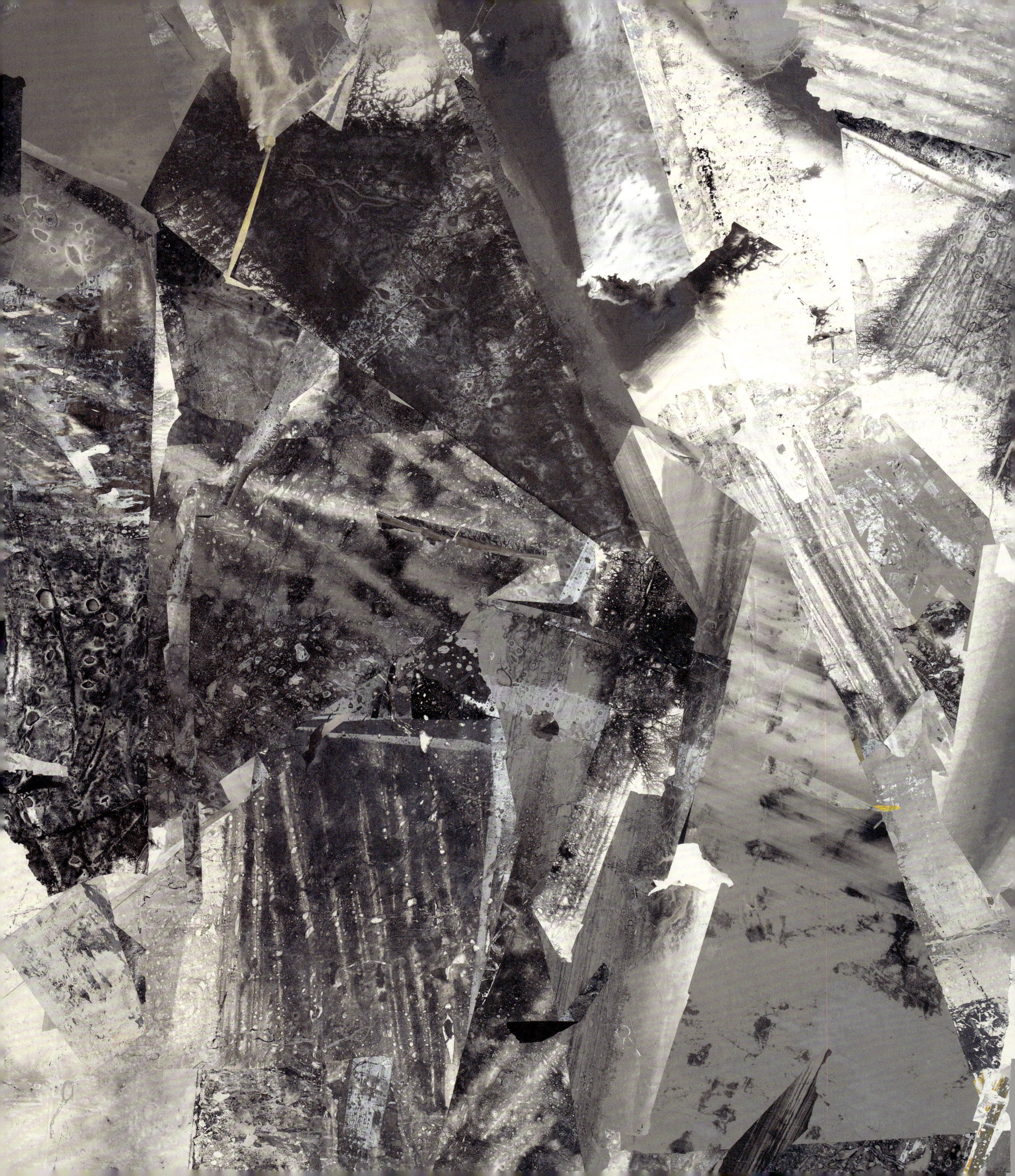

Foreword

Since first meeting Chongbin, I've come to understand his practice as deeply connected to philosophy, both Eastern and Western, and the natural landscape of our shared home state of California. His thought process is unique but relatable, rooted in a firm grasp of the physical properties and agency of nature. Often, our conversations have surrounded the art of Southern California—in particular, the Light and Space artists he has learned from.

From its inception, LACMA has been a home for Light and Space art. In 1966, just a year after opening its doors on Wilshire Boulevard, the museum hosted a two-person show featuring the works of Kenneth Price and the Light and Space master Robert Irwin. The latter's *Miracle Mile* is now a permanent fixture of the first floor of the Broad Contemporary Art Museum (BCAM) at LACMA. Over the past decade, the museum has renewed its commitment to artists working in light and space, hosting solo exhibitions for James Turrell (2013–14), Helen Pashgian (2014), Diana Thater (2015), and Mary Corse (2019). It is a distinct pleasure to host an artistic dialogue between these innovations and those of Zheng Chongbin in this solo presentation.

Support for this exhibition has been overwhelming, both within California and around the world. My deepest thanks go to Dora and Gérard Cognié, for their generous promised gift of the Fondation INK Collection, a group of more than four hundred works in the spirit of ink art, to LACMA's holdings. The Fondation INK's donations constitute nearly a third of the artworks in this exhibition, including the central video installation *Chimeric Landscape.* Without the support of the Cogniés, as well as fellow lenders Jennifer and Mark McCormick and Jerry Yang and Akiko Yamazaki, this exhibition would not have been possible. Additionally, I am appreciative of Craig Yee and INK Institute for their support in the production of this exhibition catalogue and Jack, Susy, and Libby Wadsworth for supporting the programming and catalogue for this exhibition. I am deeply thankful to Dominic Ng, Ellen Wong and East West Bank for their unparalleled support of Asian art at LACMA and of the museum in general. Finally, many thanks to Susanna Ferrell for her thoughtful curation and continued efforts to make LACMA a leading center for contemporary art of the Sinosphere, to Celia Yang for lending her expertise to this exhibition, and to the many other museum employees who worked to bring this project and its accompanying catalogue to fruition.

Michael Govan
CEO and Wallis Annenberg Director,
Los Angeles County Museum of Art

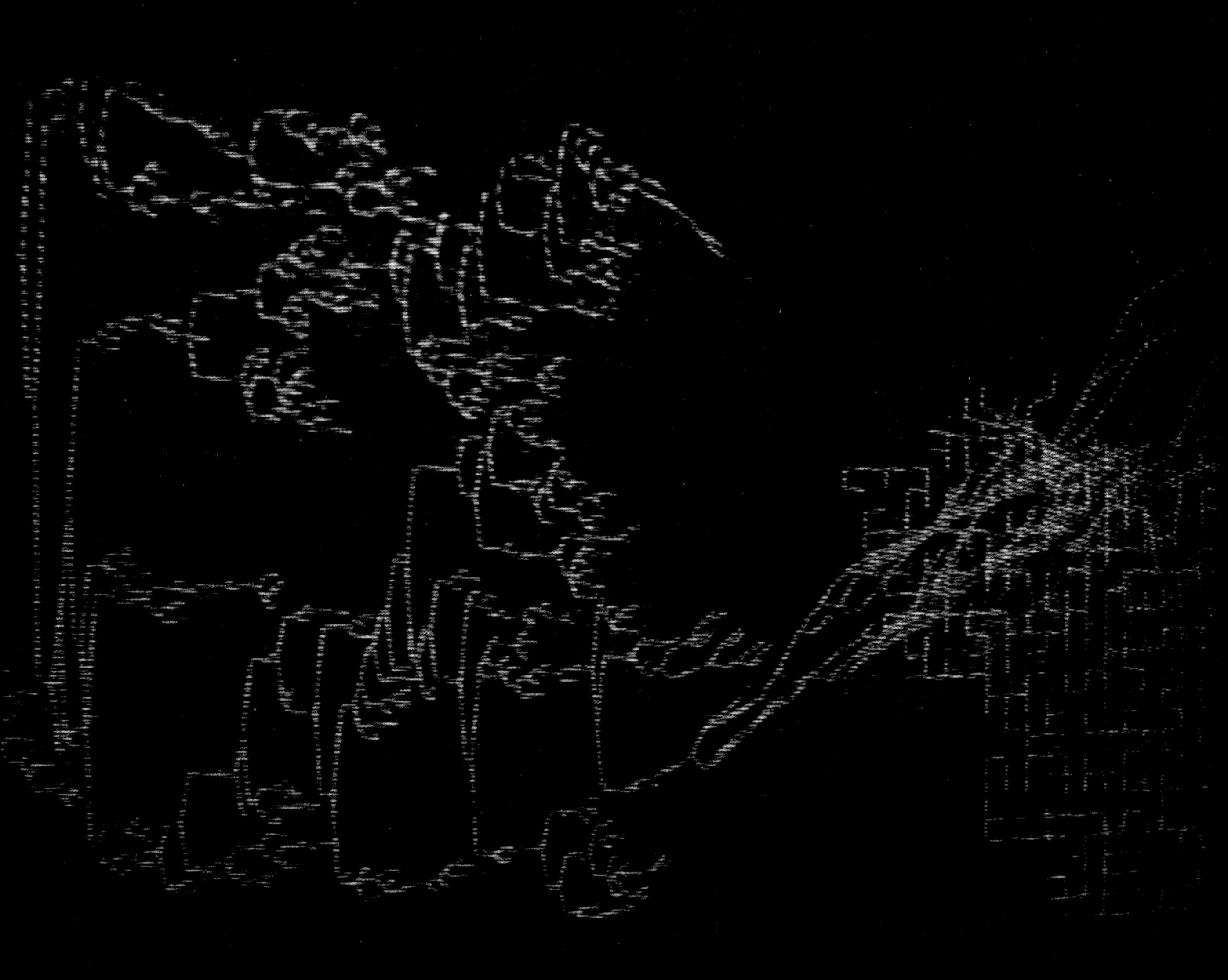

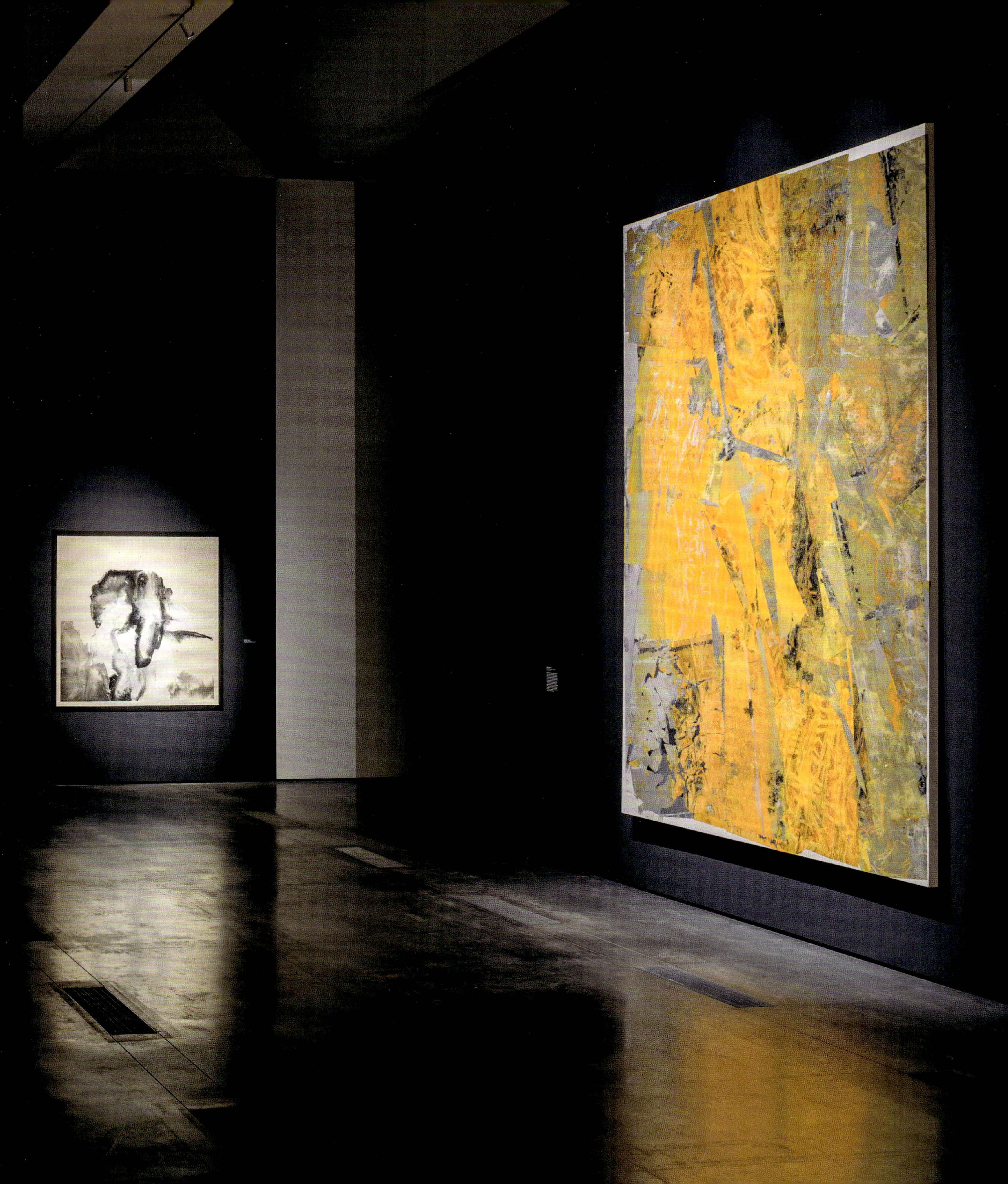

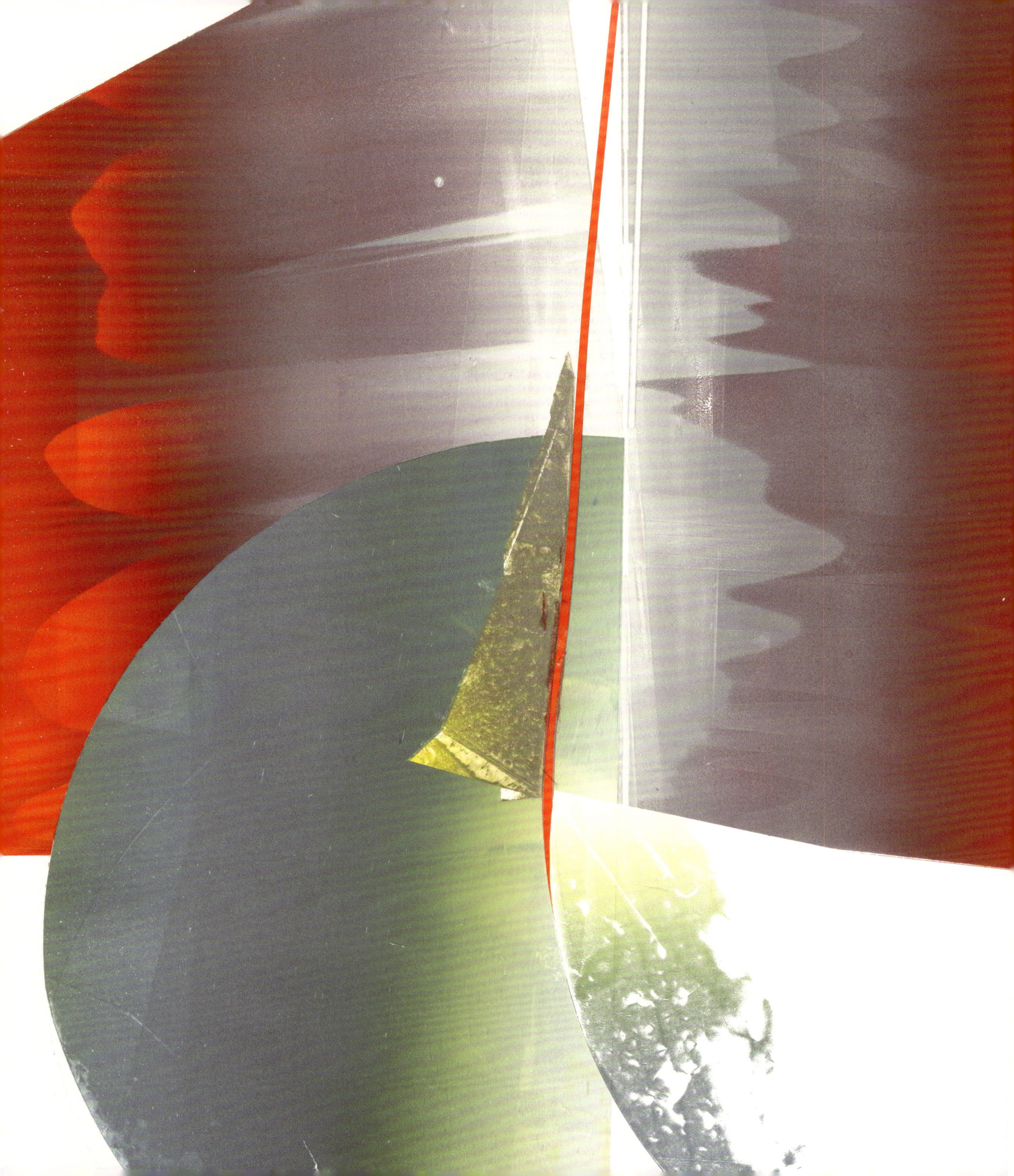

A Conversation with Zheng Chongbin

MICHAEL GOVAN

Michael Govan Let's start with the place I entered your work: somewhere between ancient and modern, between human-made and organic. When I first encountered your paintings, it was immediately evident to me how much was going on—this simple idea of oil and water, the viscous differences between ink and acrylic that created something on paper that wasn't just a depiction of nature but *was* nature. It's a hinge between ancient and modern, East and West, painting and ink. How did you come to that?

Zheng Chongbin I consider what is current and look back to the ancient. I was thinking about the material and agency, not only in terms of materiality but also as my subject. We like to perceive nature in terms of language and action: sound, movement, and sensory perceptions. This all comes from nonhuman entities, and so it has its own voice.

MG "Nonhuman," meaning natural?

ZC Right. That has its own voice, and its own integrity. In other words, if you look at nature, our construction of the imagination is always collaborative. I always feel that part of my work is influenced by Modernism and specific Modernist artists, but I never really *see* that influence. The unique imagery is because of the material, which feels almost like skin, like a membrane. These are living things. Acrylics or other media penetrate through, so the surface becomes a collaborative representation of nature. It's a presentation: it's about presenting how the other-than-human world operates and affects us.

MG   In other words, you're having a dialogue. It's not a picture of nature, it *is* nature.

ZC   Yeah. My favorite painting tradition is Song-dynasty literati painting. But for literati painters, so much of the process is understanding this whole tour through the brush in connection to the body in a very self-expressive way, which I'm starting to lose interest in.

MG   From a Western eye, you encounter things that are made from ink and associate them with the ink painting tradition. I wonder if you could sharpen those similarities, and also the differences that you're pushing away from.

ZC   I think the difference is that the brushwork of ink painting comes from a formula. Throughout history, ink painters have generalized how the brush should be used, how to paint rock formations, water, etc., so there are lots of references and indexical traces. They use these formulas to understand or learn about Chinese painting, which is very different from Western painting. I got tired of that set of frameworks, and I wanted to inject a newer vocabulary. That was the intention from the beginning, to try to break away. To try to use acrylic to dilute the purity of ink, which you're not supposed to do. It kind of trashes the ink. It's similar to Jean Dubuffet and other Western artists putting trash onto the surface of their works, changing the notion of painting. It adds physicality and is also dealing with architecture in a two-dimensional space. I felt like my work needed to be much more physical and tangible.

MG   There's an uncanny affinity between how your paintings look and how a river looks, or how an aerial picture of a mountain looks with all the crevices and fractalized edges. And you're enacting that, right? I think of it sometimes almost geologically or naturally, that you're enacting some of nature in fast motion, some of that sense of time. Is that fair?

ZC   That's true. I see the way everything's related and correlated. I study and investigate my surroundings and how those surroundings are constantly evolving. We're enacted by nature because we're being affected by its constant changes. This constant evolution constitutes our living, which I see as a collaborative process. There are spectacular scrim-like reflections on the water's surface from built-up rippling dunes under clear water forms—a sign of traced time and action, which fascinates me. These structures redirect the rippling surface of water, which causes this vibrant net-pattern reflection (fig. 1). Reverberations like these are everywhere, and it changes the behavior of the space that surrounds us.

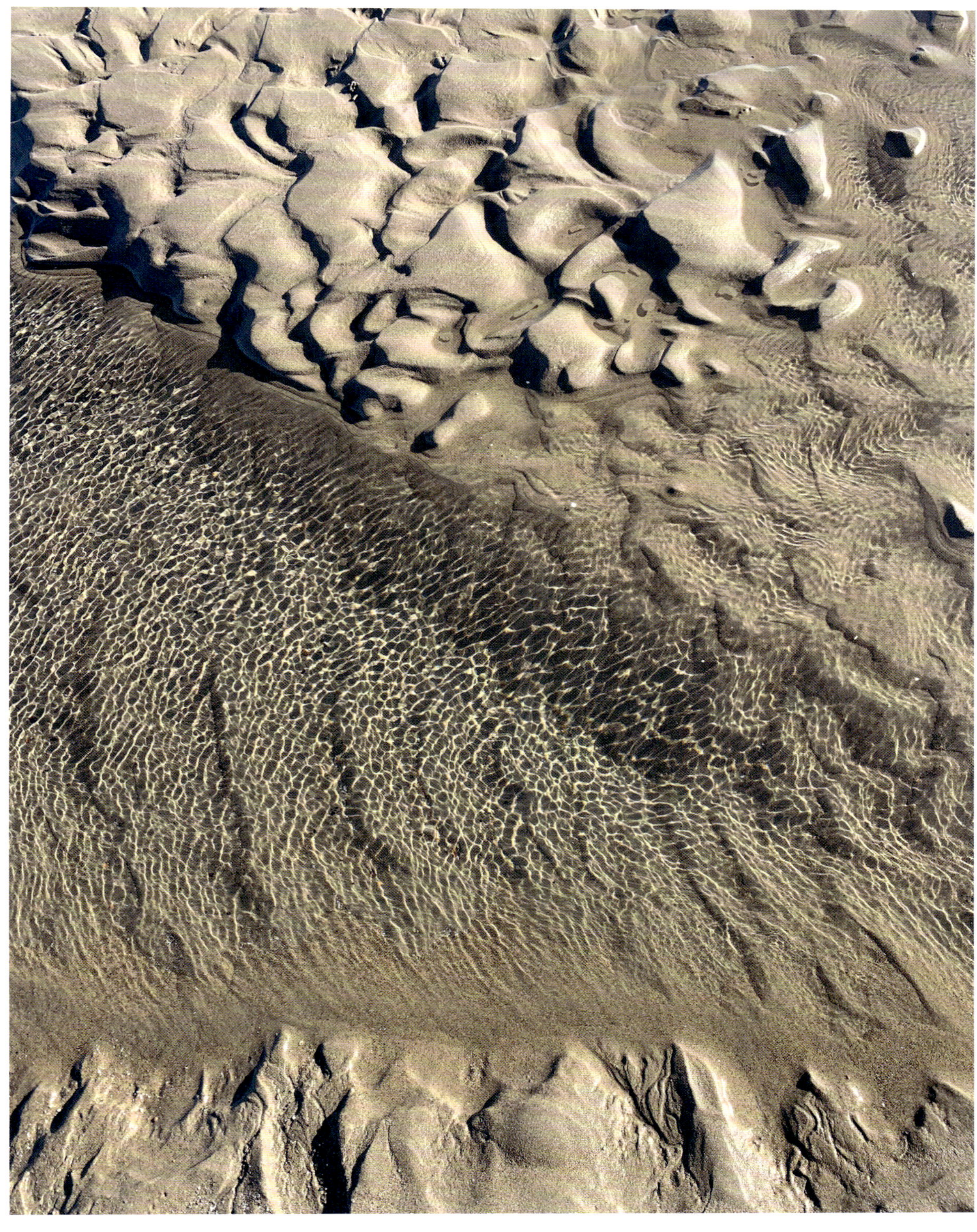

Fig. 1
A "net of light" reflected in a puddle
at Limantour Beach, Point Reyes
National Seashore, California.

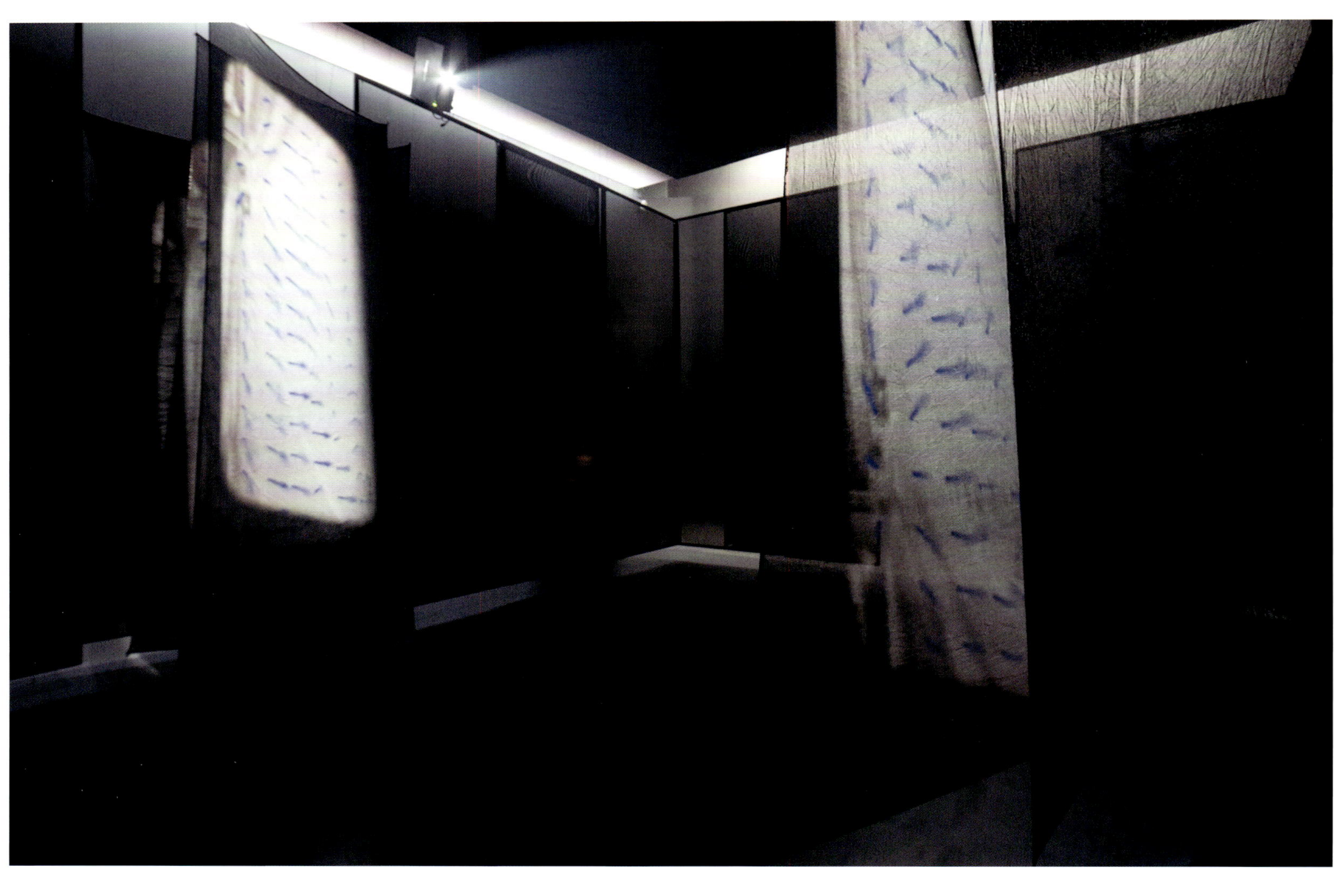

Fig. 2
Zheng Chongbin, *Walking Penumbra,*
2018. Scrim and video projection.

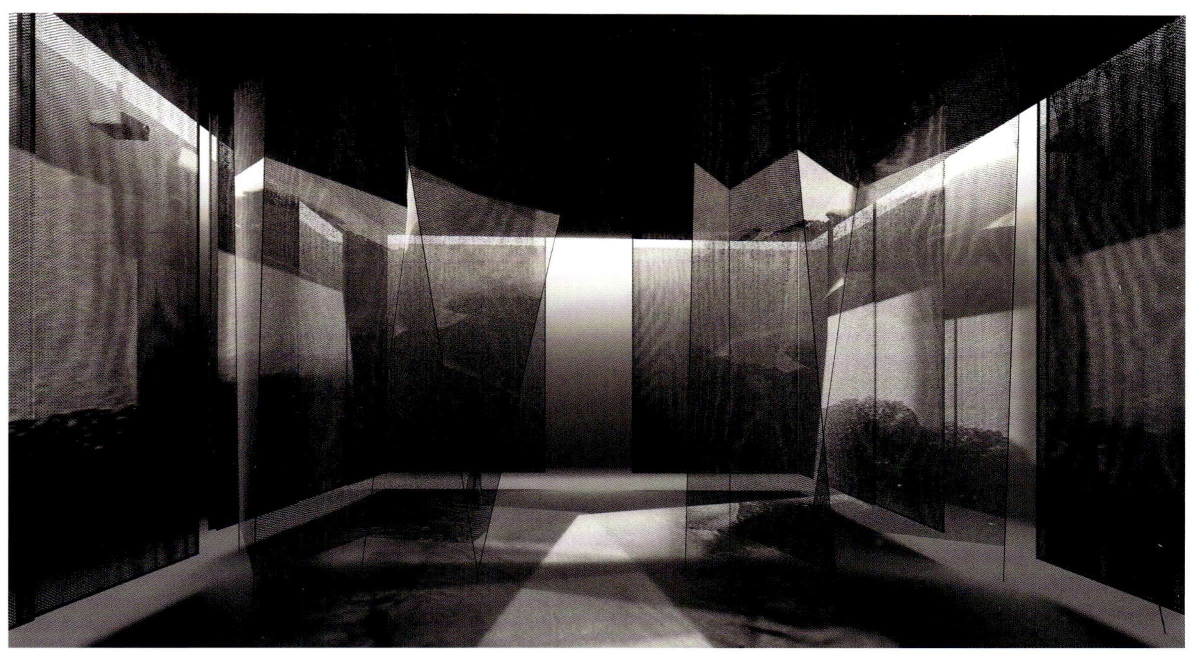

Fig. 3
Rendering of *Walking Penumbra*.

I like to compare Peircian phenomenology to the Daoist point of view.[1] I was trained in Chinese painting, and the core value to me has always been teaching you how to perceive the world, and thinking about what you want to grasp. There is this idea of capturing something that can never have a definite meaning, as the meaning has to be continuously qualified and regenerated.

But I'm also fascinated with the effectiveness of biologies, changing structures and hidden elements that modulate how we act. I learned a lot about this from acting directly in nature and thinking about how connected we are, versus when I'm in the studio and I look at materials. So it's a very *living* situation, more than thinking, "Oh, I'm producing paintings."

MG There are some overlaps between Daoism and Western phenomenology. In your art, it's easy to see the hand and the body managing ink, managing dimension, managing the flow of paint. There's a closeness between aspects of Western abstraction and ink painting that you're playing with all the time.

ZC I think that's the fun part of it, because I don't know *what* it is. Only through doing it do I find a lot of possibilities. I work on one body of work to the point that I feel that I get it, and then I get tired of it and switch to other media. It keeps me going. There is a synergy in hybridity.

MG When I first started seeing your works, you were using very modern and industrial materials in order to achieve sharp angles and three-dimensionality. Then you very poignantly added technology, and not in a hidden way, but very obviously. Can you say something about that moment?

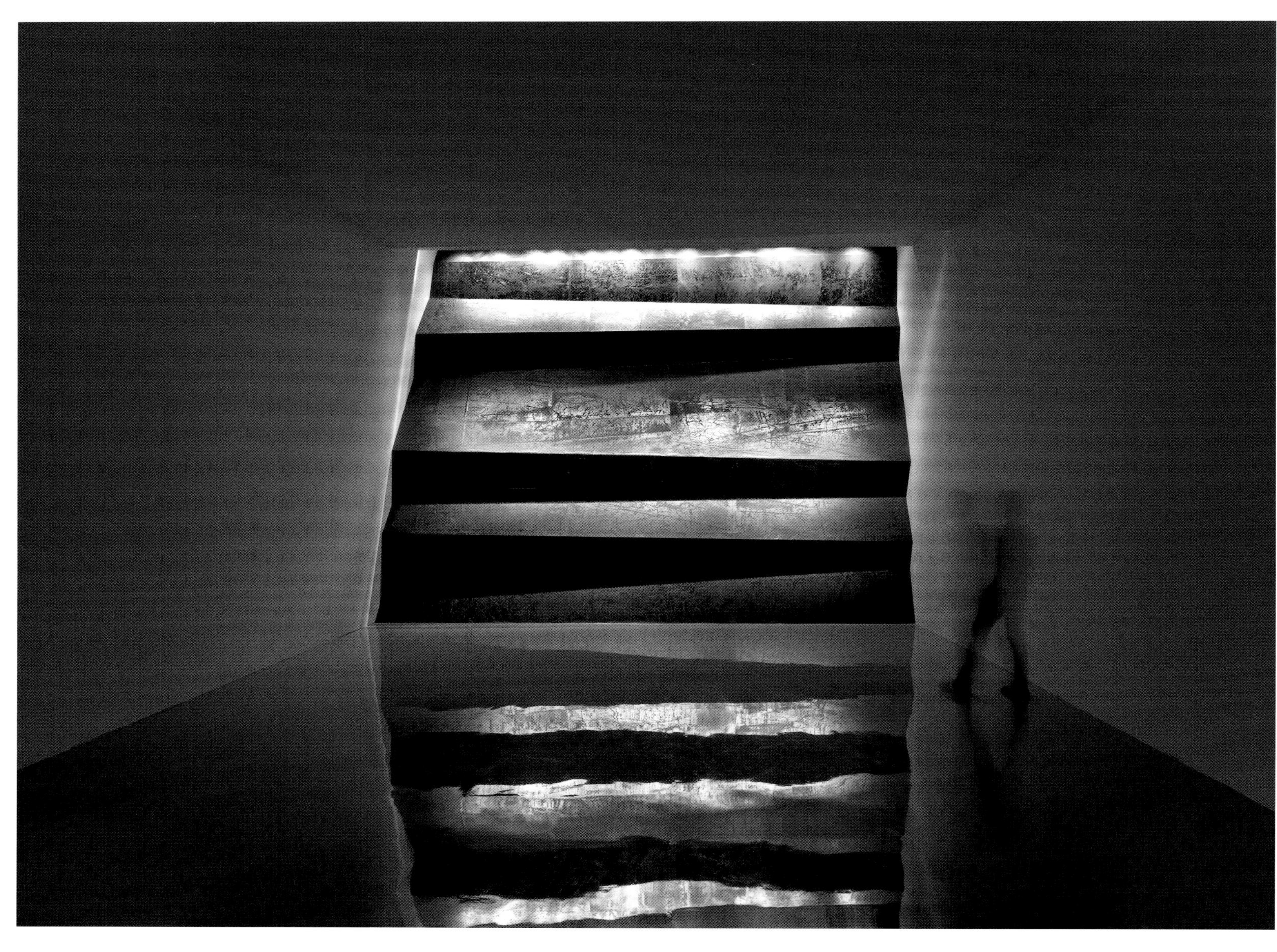

Fig. 5
Installation view of Zheng Chongbin,
Wall of Skies, 2014, light and space
installation at Ink Studio, Beijing.

I realized that a fundamental aspect of California's light is that it is very transparent, very breathable. I can see the clarity and vibrance of the light through the shadow. All of these works are defined by where I live, California—place and geography have always added meaning to existence. The connections to Light and Space work might not be so obvious if I lived on the East Coast. Tell me where you live in the landscape—I can tell who you are.

MG You spent a lot of time in China and you go back regularly, but your home is California. One of your works, *Golden State* (p. 77), seems to be a rare moment of a more literal reference—this golden state that has golden light. Has California been that place for you?

ZC Yeah, in the very tangible way that I experience the state. I realized maybe this name is because early migrants associated California with gold, especially the San Francisco Bay Area (literally "the Gold Mountain" in Chinese). I've done a lot of hiking and developed a deep connection to this land. I don't think about memories when I work on those pieces, but when putting together a piece like *Golden State*, it somehow feels like the perspective is a combination of looking at the ground and the sky. I've been assembling traces of time and space that I inherited from the California landscape. In the end, I thought about the golden state because the color is so sunny. It reminds me a lot of strata and fissures and fault lines and severed crests—all these surfaced in the structures (fig. 6). But it also feels like I'm caught in place, pushing toward the periphery with no edge. These structures don't stop; they just keep growing, growing, growing, in a rhizomatic way.

Fig. 6
Bolinas Beach, Marin County, California.

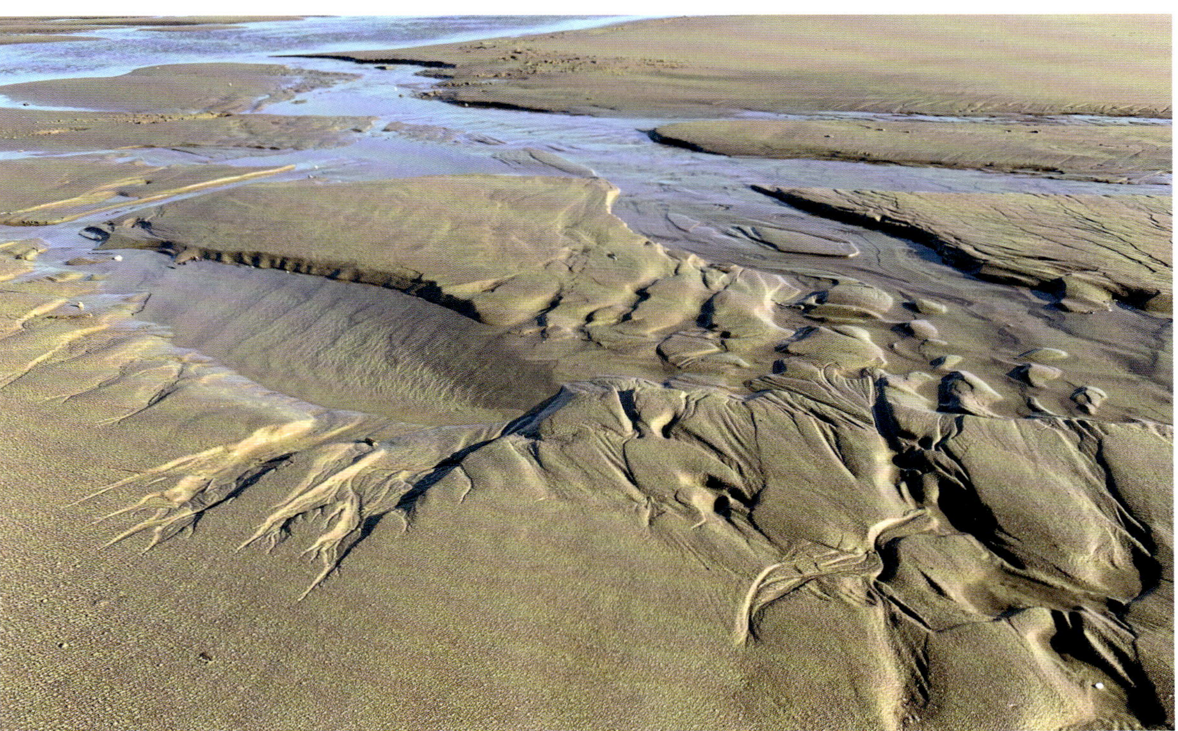

MG It's clear you're not representing a specific place, as in a bounded site or property; it's proper*ties* of experience. You've obviously spent a lot of time now with technology and light. In *Six Canons* (pp. 68–69), you come to this with a new understanding of those six historical canons of painting. How do you rethink those canons from this other point of view, in California, through technology, through your playfulness with nature?

ZC I was working on a body of work for ten years, from 2000 to 2009 or 2010, working on morphic forms, placement, and evolving growth in space. I like to use multiple sheets of paper and look at them as different places. It's like transitioning from one place to another. In a way, the imagery shifts, the formations are remade, and the fields are unsettled in a transient space. Then my work evolved to light and space, directly integrating with the environment.

During this period, I wrote a few essays about the Six Canons just for fun, because I wanted to reconceptualize them, as they are the backbone of classical Chinese painting. Everyone in history started with those guidelines. I felt that the order of the Six Canons—from most to least important—could be entirely irrelevant in terms of the context that I'm working in today, based on what I'm influenced by and study from Western contemporary art.

For example, in terms of the structures of the brushwork, dripping or throwing the rocks could be part of brushwork, so this notion of brushwork is not really limited to the brush. New techniques like cutting and folding can be repeated to deconstruct the entire work, which to me is reviewing art history. I thought about Kazimir Malevich's work and deconstruction and reforming, and about how to reorder the Six Canons based on what is relevant and what is irrelevant. The rules need to be expanded, and some actually need to be reversed.

In terms of *Six Canons*, gradually each of the pieces came to deliberately define the notion of each of the six laws—the first canon begets the second canon, the second the third, and so on. When I finished the series, I had no idea how to judge whether it was good or bad, so I left it on the wall for half a year. And the more I looked at it, the more it grew on me. Now the work is very distant from me, yet I never get tired of it. But I could never do that again.

MG It does seem that it fits some of what we were talking about before. You tend to court chance: earthquakes, fissures, moray patterns, the meeting of ink and acrylic—this sort of ambiguity. You seem to want to see what happens. You don't often come at the work with a final plan in mind.

ZC Art is not something you can be sure about. Art is something you imagine, and then when you are getting into the work it can actually lead you to different things. When I made *Six Canons*, I was very eager to think about what it means to come from that tradition, to have that DNA. Even though I've lived in California longer than I lived in China, there are core things in that tradition that I still very much connect to, consciously or subconsciously.

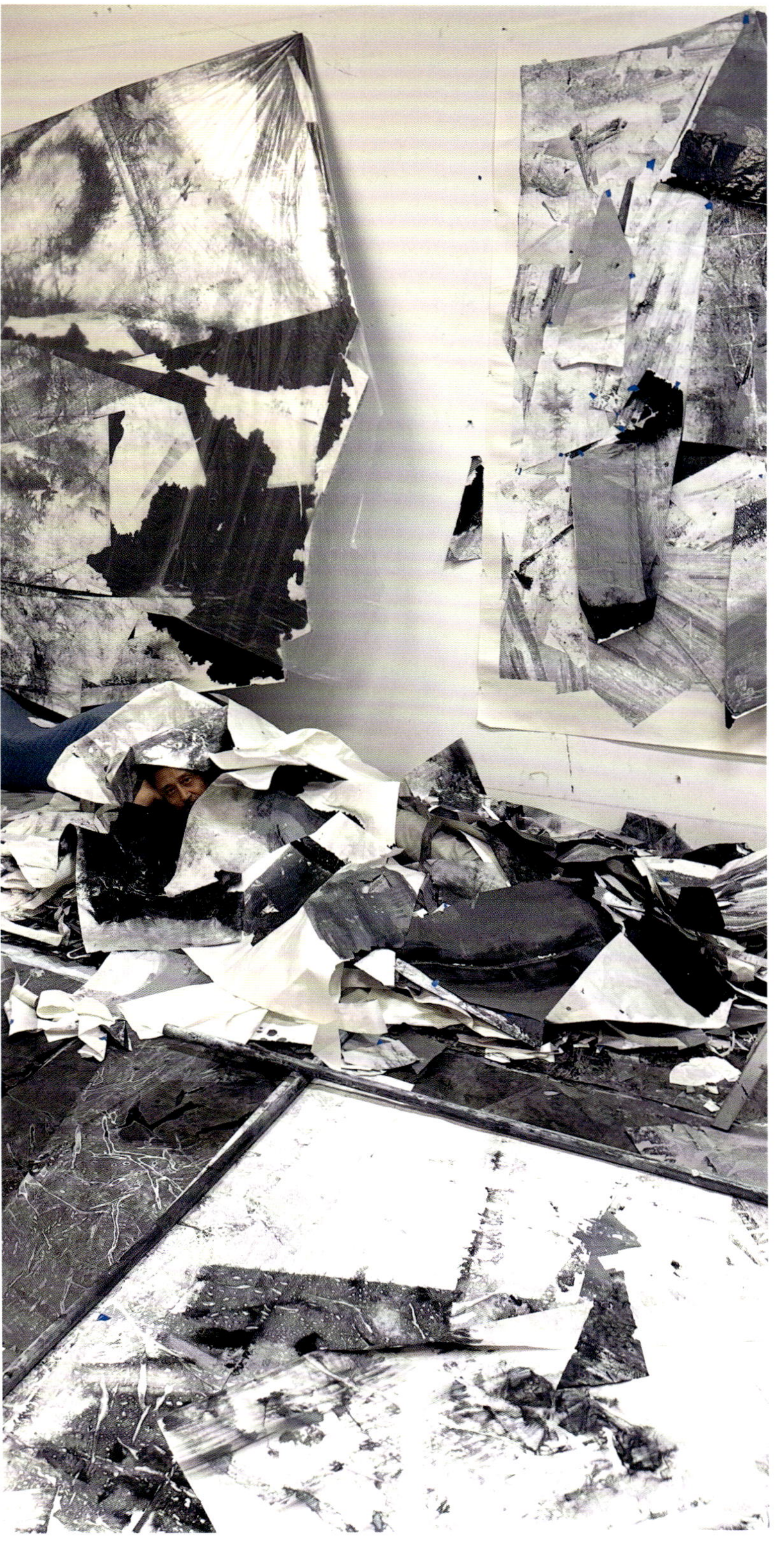

Fig. 7
Zheng Chongbin in a pile of xuan paper scraps at his studio.

It's something that literati artists like Shitao did, and I realized his theory about ink was just like Ad Reinhardt talking about black.[3] Shitao was fascinated by ink's conceptual qualities, though he didn't have the language of today. His language was still very traditional, but his idea strongly promoted materiality. I thought of him as the father of modern contemporary ink paintings. So I wrote about reinterpreting his theory, and also the Six Canons. In a way, I just wanted to get it out of my system and be done with it.

MG [Laughs] Work through it. In *Chimeric Landscape* (pp. 50–53), you have video as light and nature, and nature then looks like your paintings. Can you say something about the conception of that work?

ZC Every entity has self-organizational abilities, and I wanted to create something with actual live shots of that phenomenon or the animation of it. *Chimeric Landscape* basically weaves a whole landscape out of real/unreal, human/nonhuman things; it's a nonlinear narrative.

MG Everyone now talks about generative art, art that starts in one place and becomes something else, but I guess nature is the ultimate in generative art. There's a system of rules that then create all these images.

ZC That's true. When I filmed the scene in *Chimeric Landscape* where ink moves on the paper, I thought about how that movement embodied many things, like erosion, reorganization, regeneration, even in myself—all of these processes of becoming. I often think about why I still stick with the xuan paper (fig. 7). I heard Richard Serra say that when he worked with oil stick, he was trying to push it, and somehow the residue went to the back of his paper, which turned out to be more interesting than the front. I think of Rachel Whiteread poking holes in the paper, hoping the paint will drip through to the back side. But xuan paper is like a membrane: highly generative and coproductive. Ink can flow and grow on the surface, and also penetrate into the layers of xuan, so that the surface becomes a three-dimensional space. It's a living thing and a generative process.

MG The through line in a lot of your work is this kind of collaboration with nature, this negotiation you're always doing between materiality, physics, images of nature, chance, and this addition of light. Even the monotypes that you've been making recently have some of that same quality, because they're not fixed. They have an iridescence to them— there's movement in the materials; they're gently unstable, never fixed, creating more energy around their experience.

ZC I've only done prints in the last three years, and when I do them it feels like I'm on my break time. The monotype is something that I don't need to fully control because it relies so much on the other mechanical process. That indirect, hands-on making always excites me—I'm not the final judge of the piece. The way I think about the print is how we walk into it, how we look at it, our view. That is important to me as I think about the paintings.

MG In talking about Eastern and Western painting traditions, one of the elements you seem to be engaged with is the artist's movement, the movement of hand, arm, body. But more and more, your work relies on the *viewer's* ability to move around, to see it from different perspectives, to see an image through a screen, to move so that the iridescence emerges.

ZC Definitely, and that's a notion that is much more prominent to me since I moved here. The idea comes from the bodily experience of living here. Compared to landscape painters and classic Chinese painters, it's more about individual freedoms, and it's not so much a collective way in terms of how viewers enter into the piece. For instance, if they paint a landscape, they encourage you to walk around, not stay in one place. As a painter, you can move any hill you want to, as long as the viewer gets an idea of the whole geography and culture and site—you can construct them together to define what it is. That reflects the individual's views. But I also think it is extremely important to change that relationship to the viewer. Basically I'm dealing in my own world and then figuring out how that world can actually be seen.

MG It seems like you continue to give agency to the viewer. That's very beautiful.

Notes

1. For an introduction to Daoism, see Stephen Little, "Taoism and the Arts of China," in *Taoism and the Arts of China* (Berkeley: University of California Press, 2000), 13–31. For more on the philosophy of Charles S. Peirce, see James Jakób Liszka's *A General Introduction to the Semiotic of Charles Sanders Peirce* (Bloomington: Indiana University Press, 1996).

2. Maurice Merleau-Ponty, known for developing phenomenology in the early to mid-twentieth century. See Maurice Merleau-Ponty, *Phenomenology of Perception* (1945; London: Routledge, 2013).

3. For more on Shitao's views on painting, see Richard E. Strassberg's translation of *Huayulu* in Shih-T'ao, Richard E. Strassberg, *Enlightening Remarks on Painting* (Pasadena: Pacific Asia Museum, 1989), 61–91. A collection of Ad Reinhardt's writing can be found in Barbara Rose, ed., *Art-as-Art: The Selected Writings of Ad Reinhardt* (1953; Berkeley: University of California Press, 1991).

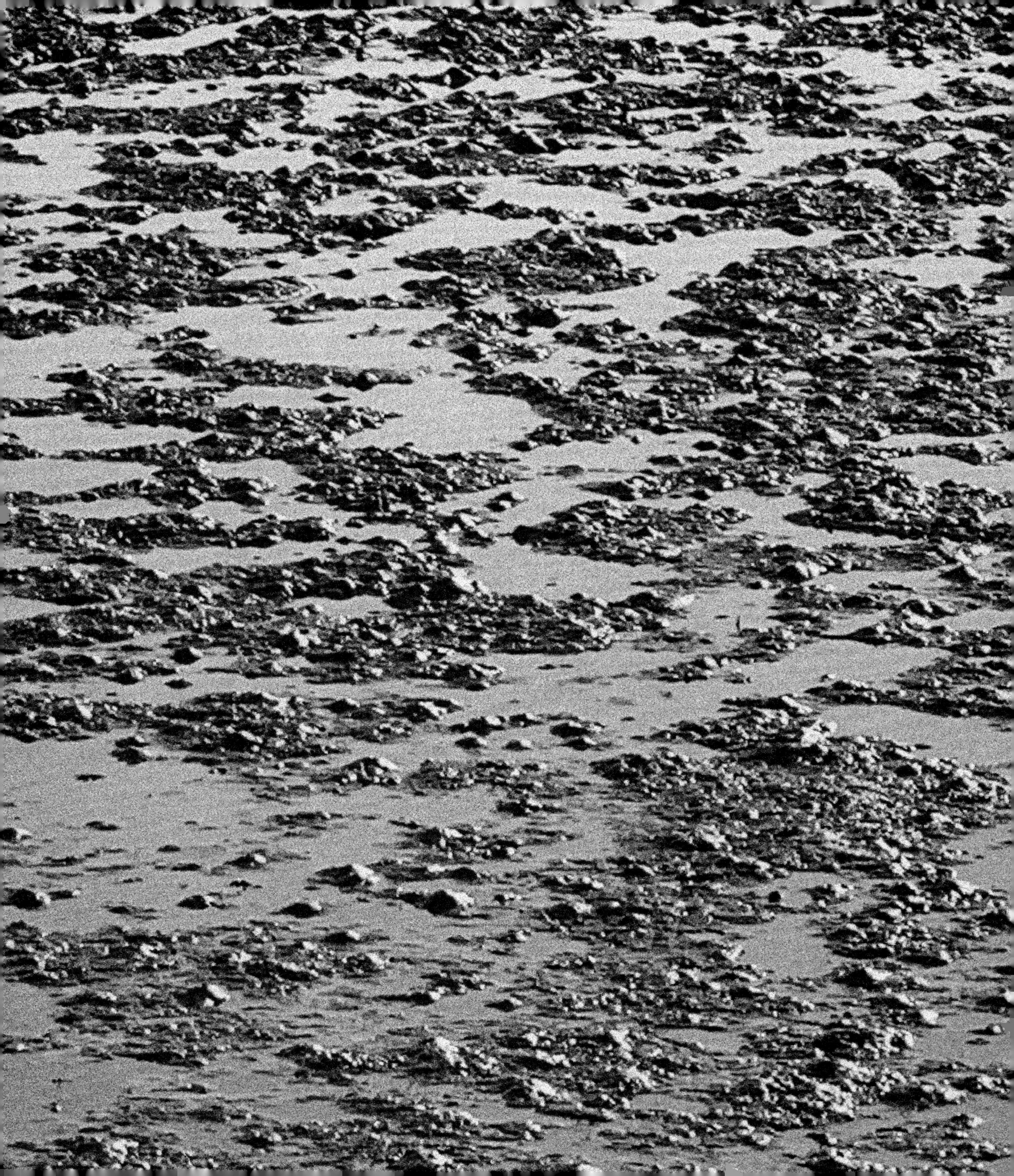

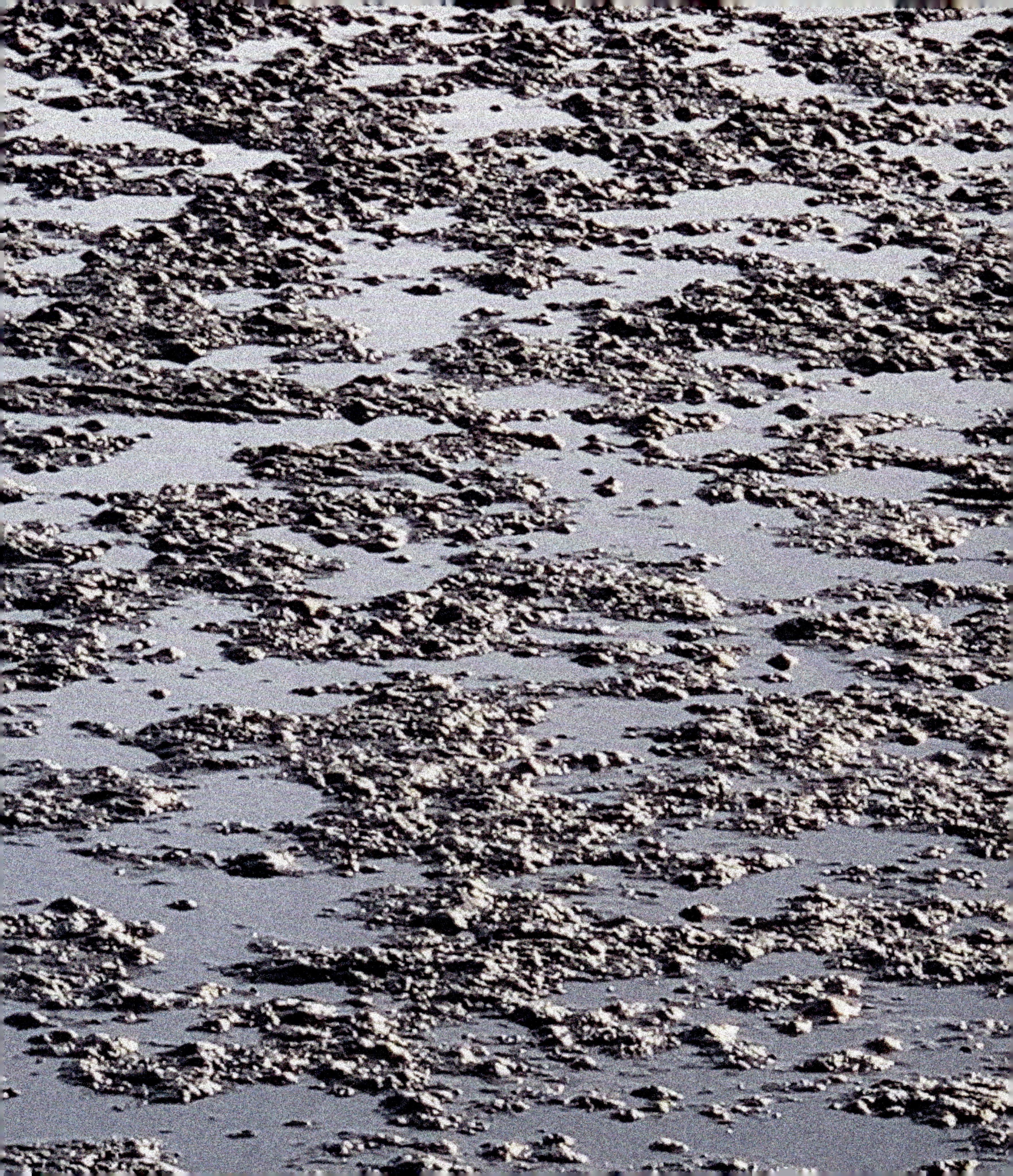

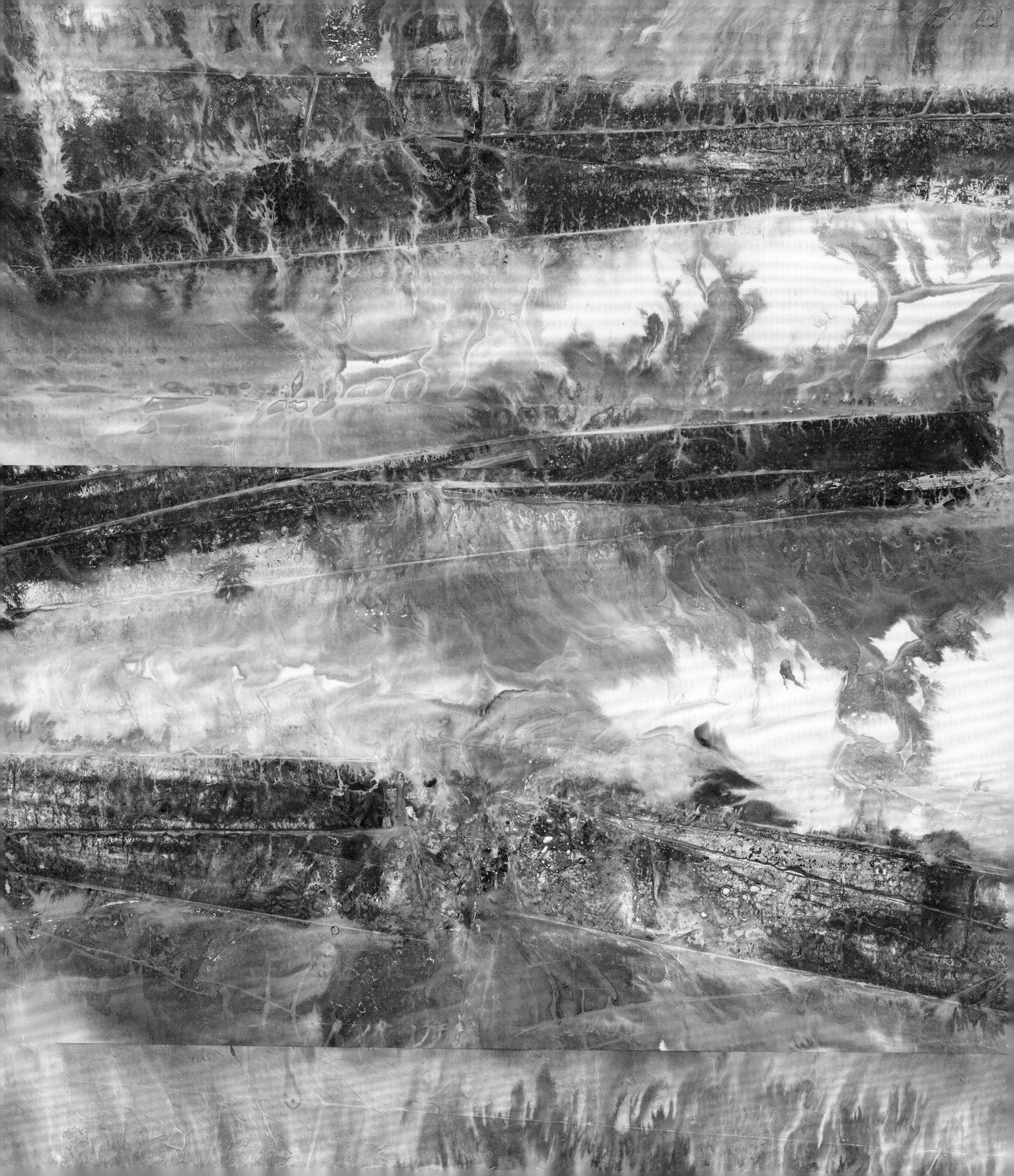

SUSANNA FERRELL

Light, Space, Land, Water

The material that I use, it's kind of a living thing … it has its own phenomenon that I want to collaborate with.

In August of 1988, Zheng Chongbin began his life in California, the state of golden hills, rocky mountain ridges, and winding rivers that he would come to know as his artistic collaborator. Zheng had studied traditional painting at the Zhejiang Academy of Fine Arts (now the China Academy of Art) in Hangzhou, and he stayed on as a professor in the late 1980s. Separating for the first time from his homeland of nearly thirty years, his painting practice underwent a major shift: "When I first arrived in the Bay Area, I felt that what I did in China was over."[1]

Zheng was honored as the first person to receive the international fellowship at the San Francisco Art Institute (SFAI), and he remained in California following his graduation from the installation and performance master's program in 1991. Throughout his time at SFAI, he was exposed to the work of countless American artists that compelled him to consider control, and loss of control, in his own practice, from Franz Kline to Cy Twombly (fig. 1). During his early years in San Francisco, Zheng was inspired by both Land artists in his master's program and those prominent in the Land art scene. He began thinking about the history and life of the land around him: what it had experienced, how it had responded, and the long-term effects. He worked closely with classmate Mark Brest van Kempen, whose *Column of Earth and Air (Free Speech Monument)* (1992; fig. 2), embedded in the ground of Sproul Plaza at the University of California, Berkeley, commemorates

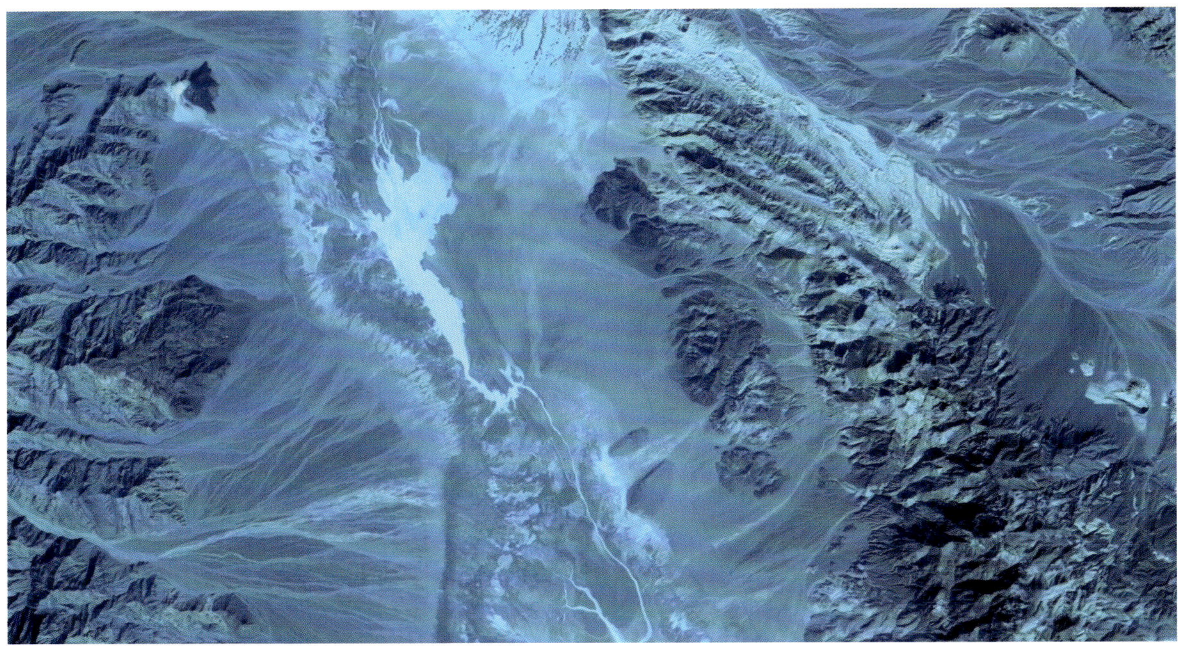

Many of these pieces expand the genre of Land art to land *and water* art, reliant upon the agency of water and its tendency to flow to create on paper a landscape consistent with an aerial view of the earth. Unique to ink is the quality of flowing in the same way as water, and the capturing of water's movement in time through evaporation. Ink is not *imitating* the appearance or movement of water, it is *being* water—it is the water within the ink that dictates how it flows. In the painting of waves, ink makes a particularly suitable medium because

Fig. 6
Still from *Chimeric Landscape*, 2015 (see pp. 50–53), showing the Sierra Nevada mountains from above.

Fig. 7
Shitao, *10,000 Ugly Inkblots*, 1685. Ink on paper, 10 × 89⅜ in.

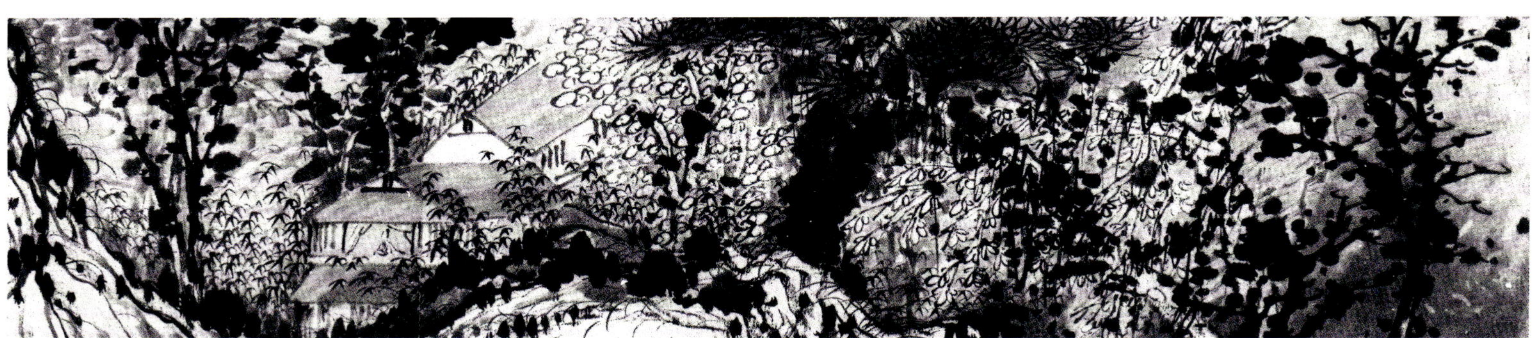

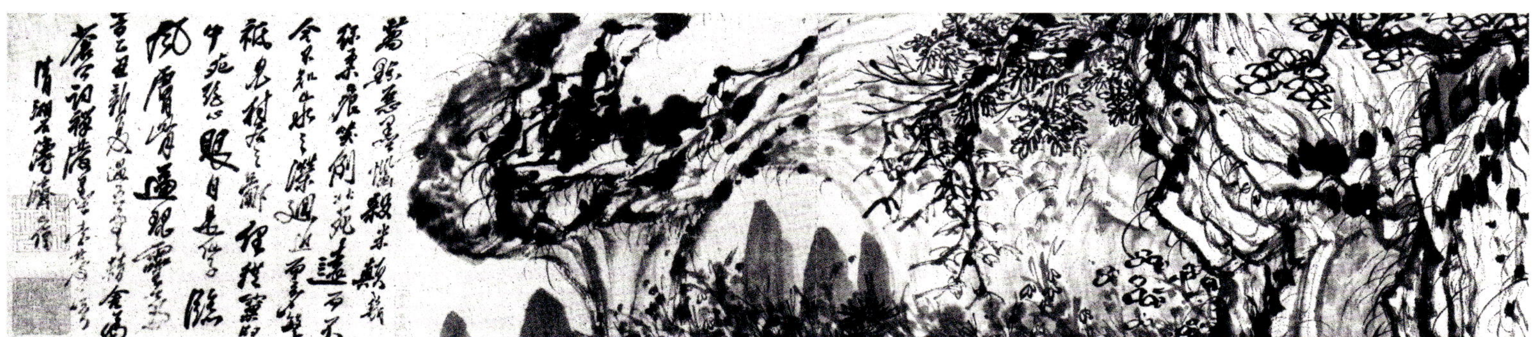

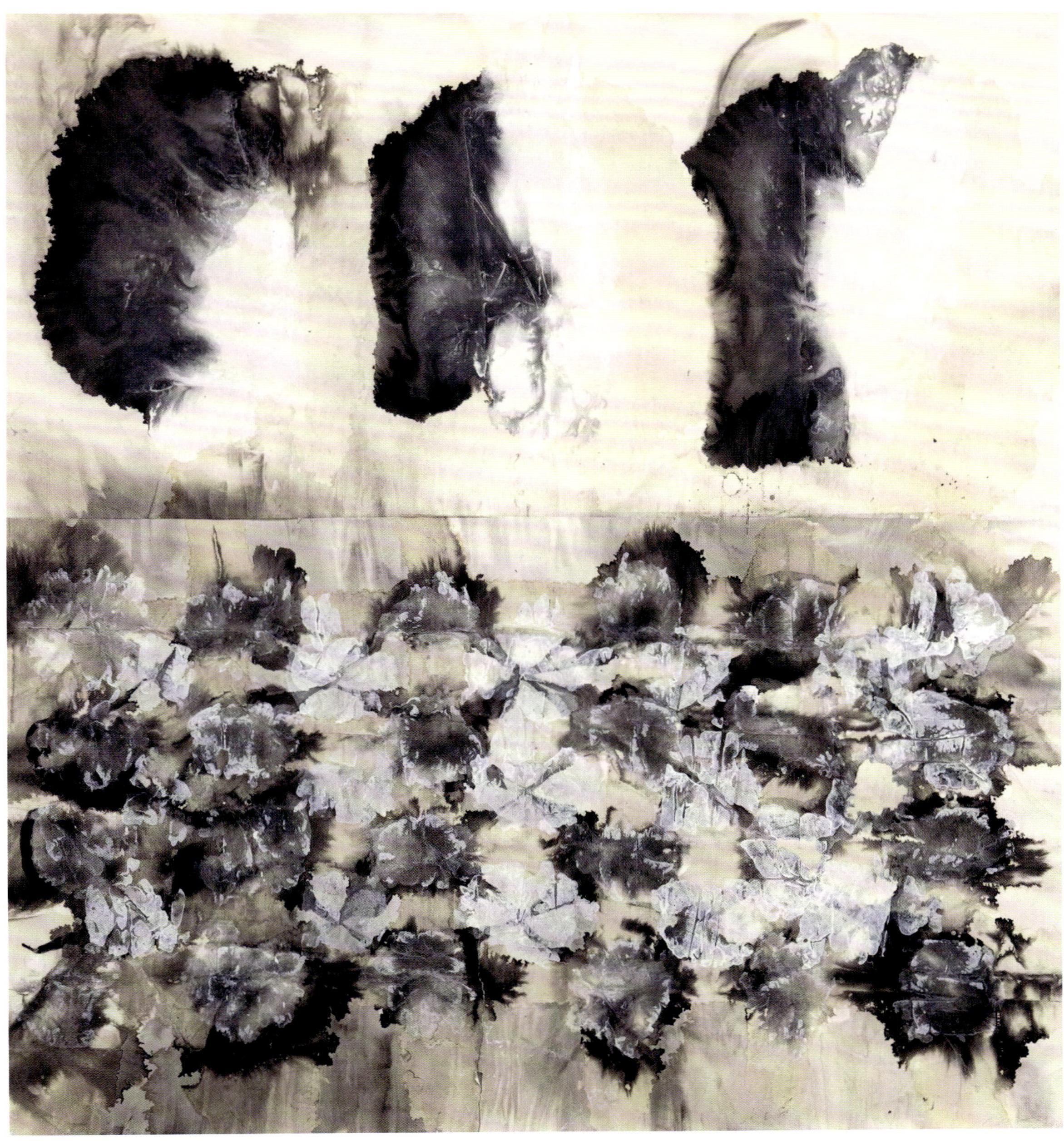

Fig. 8
Zheng Chongbin, *Blot no. 5*, 2000.
Ink and acrylic on xuan paper,
66⅞ × 63 in.

it is composed of the very thing that it is being used to depict. What remains is the impression of this movement—the ghost of the water's flow and energy; and while this is much weaker than the force of an actual current, the inherent properties of water remain constants in the depiction and its source of inspiration.

In an early iteration of his current conceptual ink practice, Zheng synthesized his Western abstract-artist inspirations with the work of Chinese literati artist Shitao (1642–1707; fig. 7), who relinquished control of the brush with his splattered-ink technique, allowing for spontaneity and chance. In the *Blot Series* (fig. 8), Zheng likewise ceded agency to his materials and the laws of physics, letting gravity, the ink's propensity to flow, and acrylic's natural properties dictate the

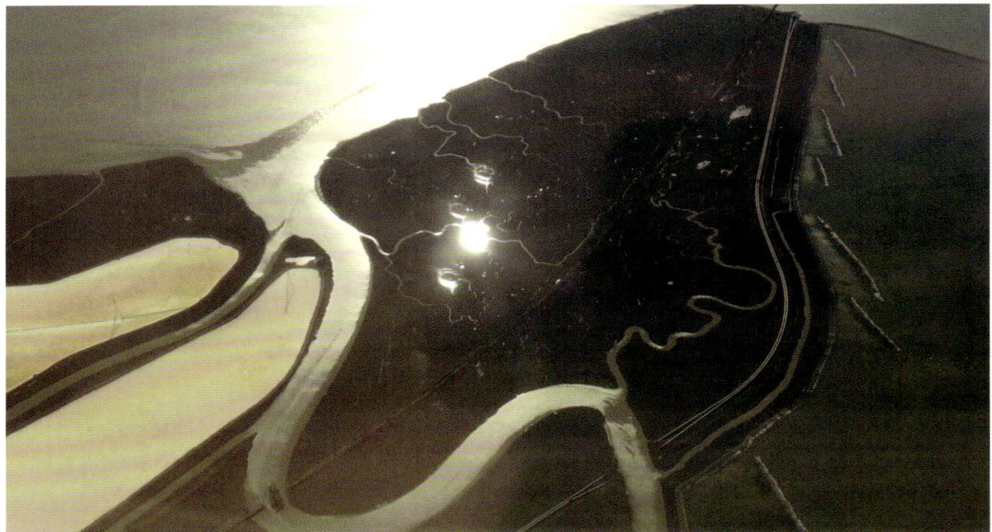

Fig. 9
Still from *Branches Are Roots in the Sky*, 2016. Video with color and sound on Betamax cassette tape. Duration: 15 min. Los Angeles County Museum of Art, Purchase with funds provided by Susan Stockel (M.2018.154).

terms of engagement. The result is a study of the physical interactions between ink and acrylic. Ink, a hydrophilic medium, runs in certain places and is forced to stop in others, where it meets the resistance of acrylic paint, a hydrophobic medium. Here and in later works, the artist accepts unpredictability. Folding, unfolding, and flipping the paper as he paints, Zheng lets the ink and acrylic conjure their own effects on each sheet of xuan.

Though perhaps most closely connected to environmental art, the process behind Zheng's paintings resonates with the principles of the Light and Space movement, which also became a significant source of inspiration for the artist after his arrival in California. The translucency inherent in Zheng's chosen xuan paper, combined with the practice of painting on both sides of the sheet, produces spectral images that show through from back to front. But it was not until the 2010s, when Zheng began to experiment with video installation, that the genres of Land (and water) and Light and Space became fully integrated within his work.

In a series of three conceptually linked videos, *Chimeric Landscape* (pp. 50–53), *Branches Are Roots in the Sky* (fig. 9), and *Mesh* (p. 55), Zheng collected images that embody flow, change, and agency. Footage of digital root systems, running ink, and streaming blood vessels draw connections between how energy is circulated within these fabricated and organic networks, great and small, and often generate similar wavelike or fractal geometries on both micro- and macroscopic levels. While the videos emphasize the life and agency of their subjects, as they move and shift of their own accord, the viewing experience itself adds another layer of mutability. The video first becomes light shone through a projector, which then lands on a mesh scrim to create a distorted view of the original imagery. Seen from different angles, the diffracted light appears as an optical illusion of vascillating iridescent patterns, restoring dimensionality to Zheng's visuals and reminding viewers that what they are seeing is not actual nature or a real medical scan but a reproduction, edited and warped. The

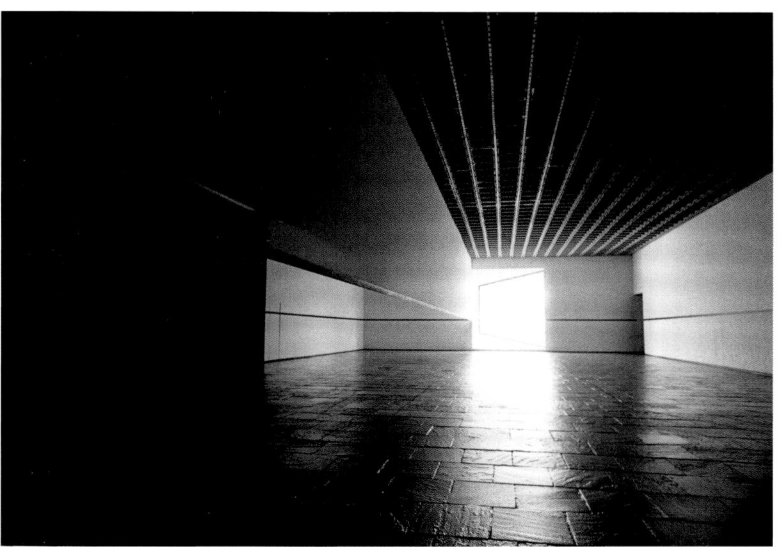

light of the projector and the mesh scrims mold one another based on their own material properties and are finally witnessed by the audience, who themselves have the agency to determine their location, angle, and time of observation. Through these elements, Zheng relinquishes control of his final artwork.

For many Light and Space artists, the desire to depict a specific image is secondary to the goal of experimenting with refractive, translucent, and reflective materials in order to push the limits of their ability to bend and absorb light. Zheng considers Light and Space artist Robert Irwin (1928–2023) an "almighty inspiration."[6] In pieces like *Scrim veil—Black rectangle—Natural light, Whitney Museum of American Art, New York* (fig. 10), a site-specific installation made in 1977, Irwin divided the space of a gallery with fine-mesh scrims, altering the overall feeling of the environment. This subtle but all-encompassing intervention into the natural light of the space, although misunderstood by visitors, represented a significant step in the history of Light and Space art. It encouraged prolonged looking and contemplation, acting as a filter for the natural beauty of changing light.

While the works of Irwin and Zheng share some physical components—the mesh scrim being perhaps the most consistent—their thinking about how the scrim simultaneously affects and reflects the natural world constitutes an even stronger alignment. For both Zheng and Irwin, the mesh scrim acts as not only a mediator but also a conductor of light. Irwin's scrims work in conjunction with natural or ambient light, effectively softening or darkening the light in a space. Zheng's mesh scrims, conversely, are used to allow the bright, focused light of a projector to permeate outward. In effect, Irwin's work is focused around the shadow created by his scrim, whereas Zheng's meshworks rely on the holes or voids in the material and the light that penetrates through them. The dark scrim is less a present object than a void, enlivened only when lit by the bright, focused light of a projector; each of its holes become an active frame, illuminated on all four sides. When viewed from afar and conceptualized as a wall or boundary, the

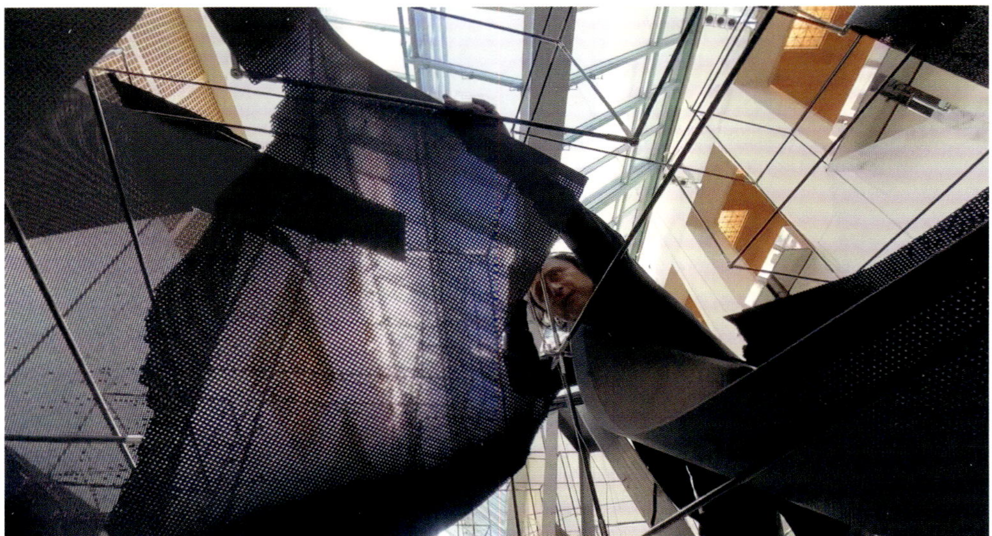

scrim becomes a way of recognizing the void, or the *absence* of boundary; it is permeable, roughly equal parts presence and absence (fig. 11).

Irwin was interested in "energy as a perceptual property": for example, the ability of a painting to direct the viewer's eye and focus, or to catalyze the brain's perception of an optical illusion. As our attention is directed around the artwork or space, the energy of that movement results in the changing imagery that we see. Zheng's work contains the additional dimension of flux: his installations can be entered at any point in the video's duration, from any angle and for any length of time, thus shifting our perception. As Maya Kóvskaya writes, "To encounter *Chimeric Landscape*, you must take an active stance, positioning yourself in relation to the images that unfold before and around you, changing aspects of what you see depending on your location."[7] She invokes the Chinese cosmological figure *hundun* 混沌, whose ever-changing visage embodies this idea of constant flux or chaos. Encompassing infinite aesthetic and perceptual experiences, works like *Chimeric Landscape* and *Mesh* engage with not only the perceptible energy and agency of the depicted materials (water, ink, flowing blood, flashing machinery and screens) but also the energy and agency of the viewer. Zheng allows for chance and the will of the viewer to define his final compositions, creating not one truth to the experience of the work, but many.

Through a range of media—ink, acrylic, paper, mesh scrim, video, water, light, and space—and attention to the agency of his materials, Zheng Chongbin creates works both unique to each viewer and echoed in landscapes around the world. His paintings and video installations understand ink, paper, and video as not only invoking but also composed at an essential level of water, land, light, and space, intersecting and influencing one another. As the conductor of these materials, Zheng makes a case for ink as water and video as light, coalescing in works that trace the energy of active matter and traverse the lines between genres.

Fig. 11
Zheng Chongbin preparing a piece of mesh scrim for his site-specific installation *I Look for the Sky*, Asian Art Museum, San Francisco, 2020.

Bibliography

Beres, Tiffany Wai-Ying. "Boundless Ink." *ArtAsiaPacific*, no. 97 (March 2016): 122–31.

Beres, Tiffany Wai-Ying and Zheng Chongbin. "Materials of Inspiration: Zheng Chongbin." *Orientations* (July/August 2017): 28–31.

Chen, Abby, and Maya Kóvskaya. *Zheng Chongbin: I Look for the Sky.* San Francisco: Asian Art Museum, 2021.

Clark, Robin, and Michael Auping. *Phenomenal: California Light, Space, Surface.* Berkeley and San Diego: University of California Press and Museum of Contemporary Art, 2011.

Claypool, Lisa. "Architectonic Ink: Zheng Chongbin in Conversation with Lisa Claypool." *Yishu: The Journal of Contemporary Chinese Art* 10, no. 4 (2011): 41–53.

Eliel, Carol S., ed. *Light, Space, Surface: Art from Southern California.* Los Angeles and New York: Los Angeles County Museum of Art and DelMonico Books, 2021.

Erickson, Britta. *Zheng Chongbin: Impulse, Matter, Form.* Beijing: Ink Studio, 2014.

Erickson, Britta, and Richard Widmer, dirs. *The Enduring Passion for Ink: Zheng Chongbin's Process*, 2016, *kanopy*, https://www.kanopy.com/en/product/enduring-passion-ink.

Kóvskaya, Maya. "Becoming Landscape: Diffractive Unfoldings of Light, Space, and Matter in the New Work of Zheng Chongbin." *Yishu: The Journal of Contemporary Chinese Art* 14, no. 6 (2015): 6–21.

Moore, Chris. "Zheng Chongbin—Myth, Matter, Medium." Translated by Qian Fan. *Randian*, December 18, 2015, http://www.randian.art/zheng-chongbin-myth-matter-medium/.

Nipper, Marie, and Nikolaj Kirke. *Light + Space.* Copenhagen and Berlin: Copenhagen Contemporary and LAS, 2022.

Yee, Craig, ed. *Zheng Chongbin: Walking Penumbra.* Beijing: Ink Studio, 2018.

Zara, Janelle. "Does It Move You? How to Look at Art, According to the Late Robert Irwin." *Contemporary Art Review.la*, June 18, 2024, https://contemporaryartreview.la/does-it-move-you/.

Notes

1. Lisa Claypool, "Architectonic Ink: Zheng Chongbin in Conversation with Lisa Claypool," *Yishu: The Journal of Contemporary Chinese Art* 10, no. 4 (2011): 47.

2. Chris O'Sullivan, "Designer Named for UC Free Speech Memorial," *San Francisco Examiner*, April 17, 1990, https://www.sfartistsalumni.org/post/1990-free-speech-monument-uc-b-by-sfai-s-mark-brest-van-kempen.

3. Zheng Chongbin, conversation with the author, November 18, 2024.

4. Zheng Chongbin, conversation with the author, November 18, 2024.

5. "2021 Incident Archive," CAL FIRE, accessed January 20, 2024, https://www.fire.ca.gov/incidents/2021.

6. Chris Moore, "Zheng Chongbin—Myth, Matter, Medium," *Randian*, December 18, 2015, http://www.randian.art/zheng-chongbin-myth-matter-medium/.

7. Maya Kóvskaya, "Becoming Landscape: Diffractive Unfoldings of Light, Space, and Matter in the New Work of Zheng Chongbin," *Yishu: The Journal of Contemporary Chinese Art* 14, no. 6 (2015): 7.

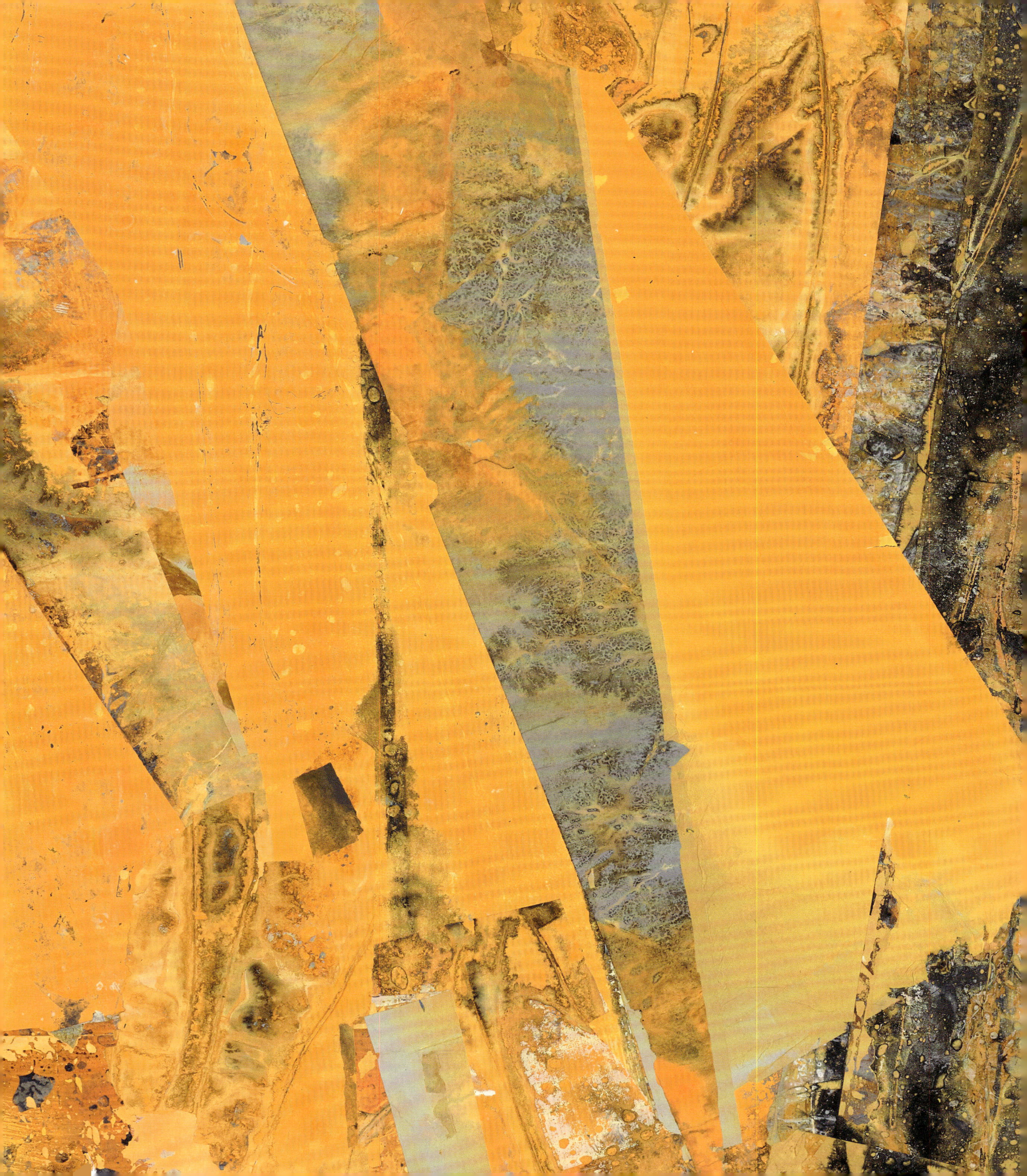

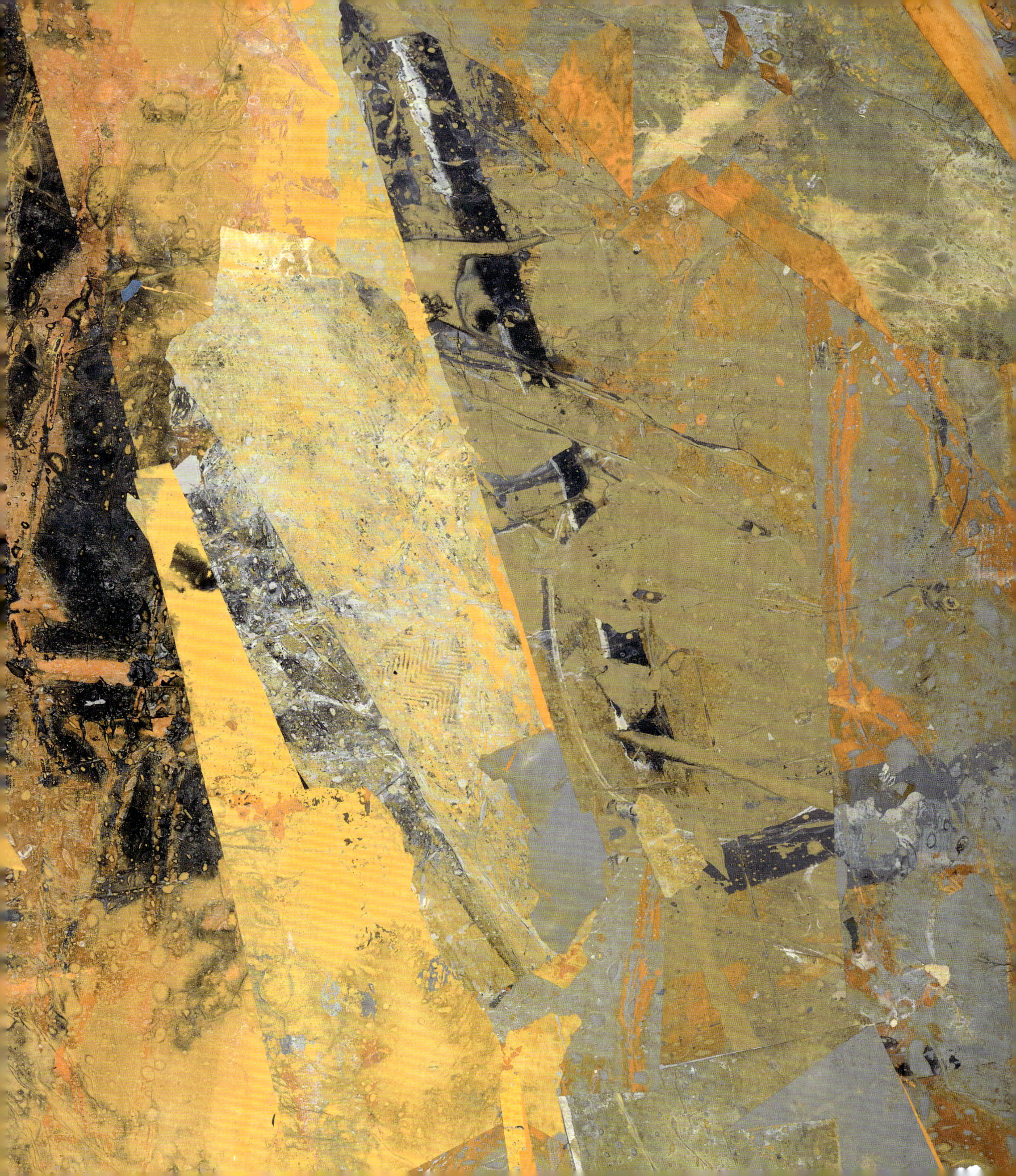

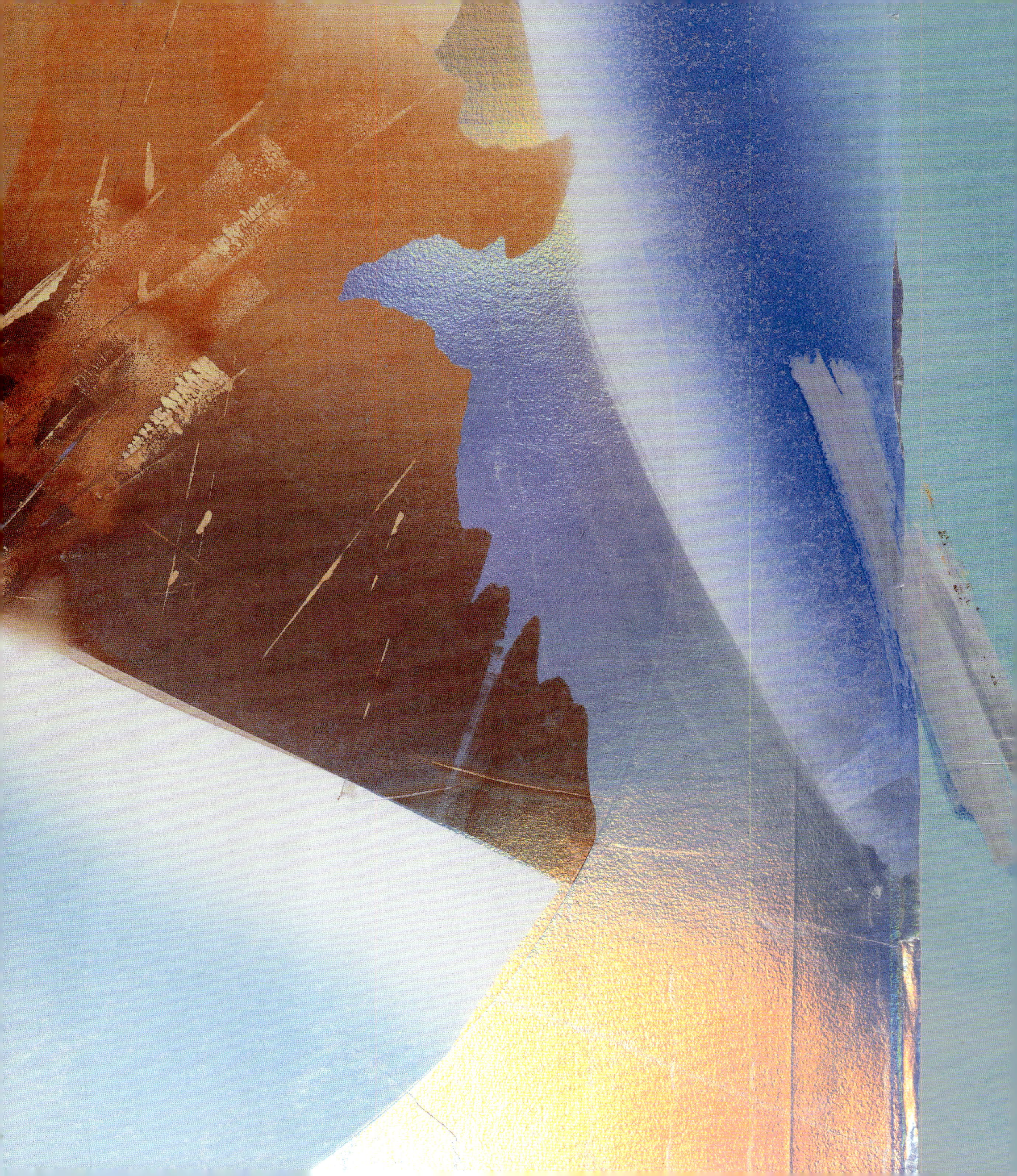

Material Fluidity in Zheng Chongbin's Printmaking Practice

CELIA YANG

Spherical formations echo across the surface of the paper, their reverberations a rhythmic interplay with the print's jagged geological features. These elements dance, recede, and emerge in a fluid choreography of light and shadow. Vibrant layers of color rest against expanses of pristine white space, imbuing the landscape with both energy and stillness. Directional lines, created through scraped or brushed textures within the ink, lead the viewer's gaze from left to right, evoking the flow, or *qiyun*, of Chinese ink painting.[1] In scale and format as well, *The Poetry of Receding Continents* (2024; p. 89) recalls that tradition, a cornerstone of Zheng Chongbin's early training at the Zhejiang Academy of Fine Arts. Circular motifs suggest astral bodies, while the serrated edges of layered paper summon the rugged contours of landforms. Zheng's monotype embodies a harmonious tension between symmetry and opposition, existence and emptiness, the terrestrial and the celestial. Untethered from linear notions of time or space, it materializes core Daoist principles, embracing the balance of opposites and the interconnectedness of all things, but creating a new form of the timeless landscapes it references.

Yet it is the work of eighteenth-century Italian artist Giambattista Tiepolo that inspired *The Poetry of Receding Continents*. Zheng first encountered Tiepolo's paintings in the 1990s during a trip to Italy, but it was not until he began experimenting with printmaking that he truly delved into a study of the master's technique. "I love how he paints so loosely, with such freedom," Zheng recalls. "He is such a great colorist, able to put two unexpected colors together to create dynamism."[2] Zheng was specifically drawn to the color strategies Tiepolo employed

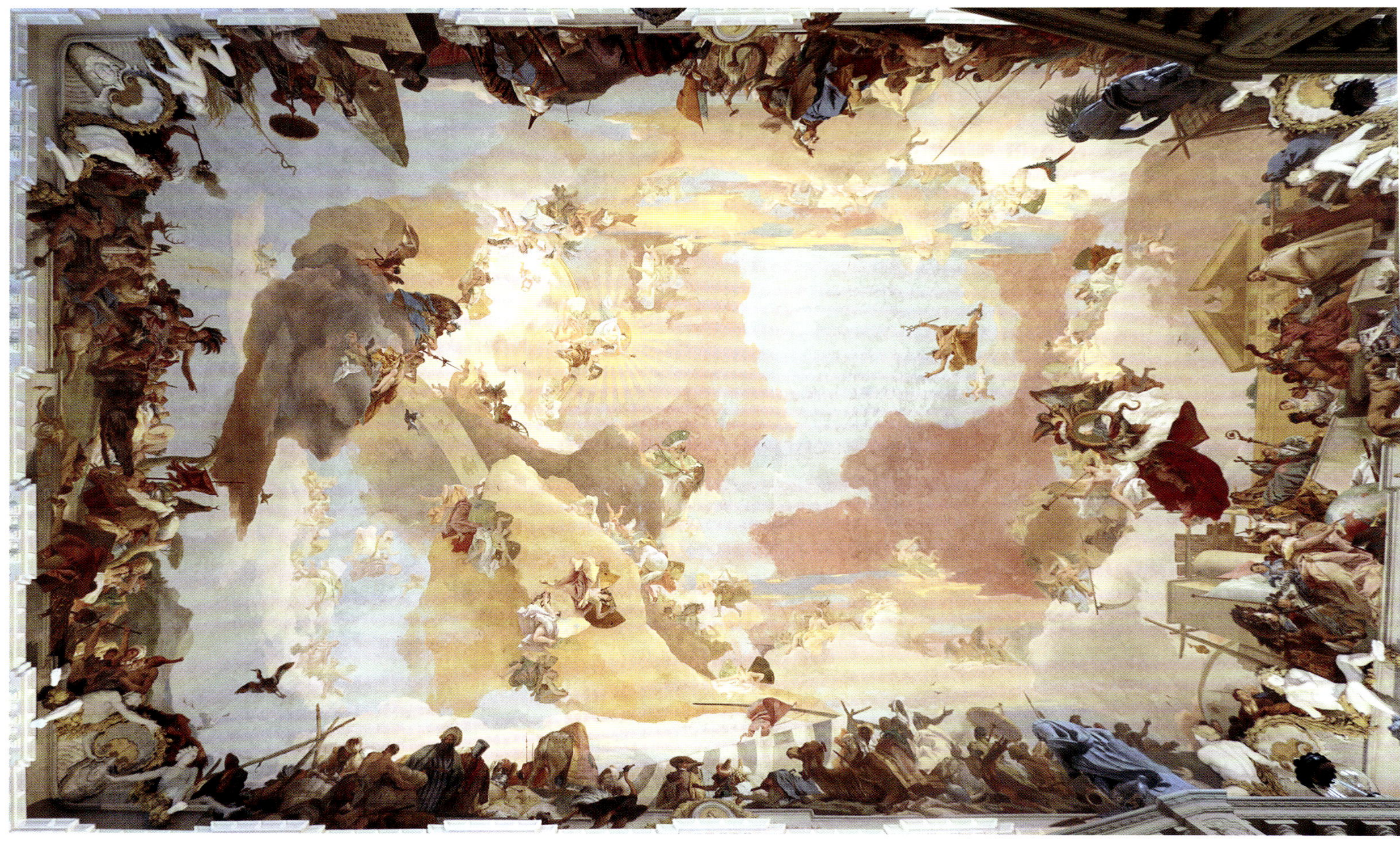

for the ceiling fresco *Allegory of the Planets and Continents* in the Würzburg Residenz in Germany (fig. 1), using tones to create lumination, spatial depth, and movement. *The Poetry of Receding Continents* exudes the same glowing, atmospheric quality as Tiepolo's fresco, an effect Zheng achieved by blurring colors with tints, variations in printing pressure, and the layering of iridescent paper. Carefully applying colored ink onto paper, Zheng selectively removes portions of it through a process of rubbing, wiping, and brushing away. This technique produces angular, blurred lines that merge and soften the forms of color, gradients, and discreet edges that enhance the work's ethereal radiance. Contrasting warm and cool tones generate spatial tension, while the iridescent paper, paired with the repetition of lines and shapes, evokes a sense of kinetic energy. Transparent, overlapping formations simulate light passing through layers, creating a lively interplay between light and shadow. As the viewer approaches the work from different angles, the image shimmers and changes like a lenticular print. The resulting work feels weightless yet monumental, an evocation of immense tectonic and cosmic spectacle.

Zheng conceived *The Poetry of Receding Continents* in the shop of master printmaker Kathryn Kain. Nestled in an old shipyard on the San Francisco Bay, the space faces the brilliant waters and offers an

Fig. 1
Giambattista Tiepolo, *Allegory of the Planets and Continents*, Treppenhaus, Würzburg Residenz, 1751–53, Würzburg, Germany.

unobstructed panorama of Bay Farm Island. Working collaboratively with Kain, who specializes in experimental lithography, Zheng began producing prints in the summer of 2022. His decision to add print-making to his artistic repertoire was partially motivated by exposure to Larry Bell's multidimensional works on paper, but also by his own desire to reintroduce color to his practice. Zheng fully embraced the spontaneity and immediacy of the printing process and its inherent invitation to experiment. Favoring monotypes, he works at a steady, meditative pace, starting and restarting ideas, drawing inspiration from art-historical references, the studio's striking, light-filled vistas and surroundings, and his keen observations of the human experience. His approach to creating a monotype is labor-intensive, as he meticulously explores the possibilities of the lithography process.

Much like in his painting practice, Zheng defies the rules of printmaking. He allows the materials themselves—the paper, ink, and even the natural elements drifting through the studio—to dictate the outcome. Zheng uses various grades of paper, newsprint, and even iridescent materials to study how they influence optical properties. He intentionally runs the press on paper with varying degrees of moisture to explore how different absorbencies affect the ink's ability to bond with the paper. He presses over impressions that have not fully dried. He combines solvents with the ink, testing its molecular properties and immiscibility. Dust and filament drifting through the studio leave subtle, fossil-like imprints. He is not confined by the limitations of the size of the press and will collage prints to form larger compositions. Whether through fluctuations in printing pressure, unpredictable effects from his materials, or airborne particles, Zheng sets the stage for the unexpected, reveling in the allure of the unknown.

Zheng also approaches printmaking by employing aesthetics that have proven successful in his painting practice. By working with familiar forms and techniques, such as collaging monochromatic shapes, and brushing, layering, and subtracting ink, he captures the sensibilities of light and space in his monotypes. *Aurora* (2023; p. 84) is a striking example of how Zheng transferred the qualities found in his paintings into his prints. He combined a water-based solvent with oil-based ink, creating organic, rootlike structures that emerged from the chemical reaction between the two fluids, allowing the inherent properties of the materials to unfold. Collaged forms overlap and intersect, creating layers that enhance depth and spatial tension. The monochromatic palette is rich in tonal values, ranging from deep black to brilliant white. Gradient transitions imbue the work with diffuse light and atmospheric depth, as if light itself were radiating from the surface, bursting forth in luminous cosmic splendor. The resulting composition is structured yet fractured and seemingly breaks free of the rectangular confines of the paper. Similar visual elements appear in Zheng's ink and acrylic paintings, such as *Between the Two Spaces* (2016; p. 65). Gradually, however, he began to leverage the efficient output of printmaking to experiment with color, using it as a kind of sketchbook for his paintings. As demonstrated in *The Poetry of Receding Continents*, printmaking allows Zheng to investigate how

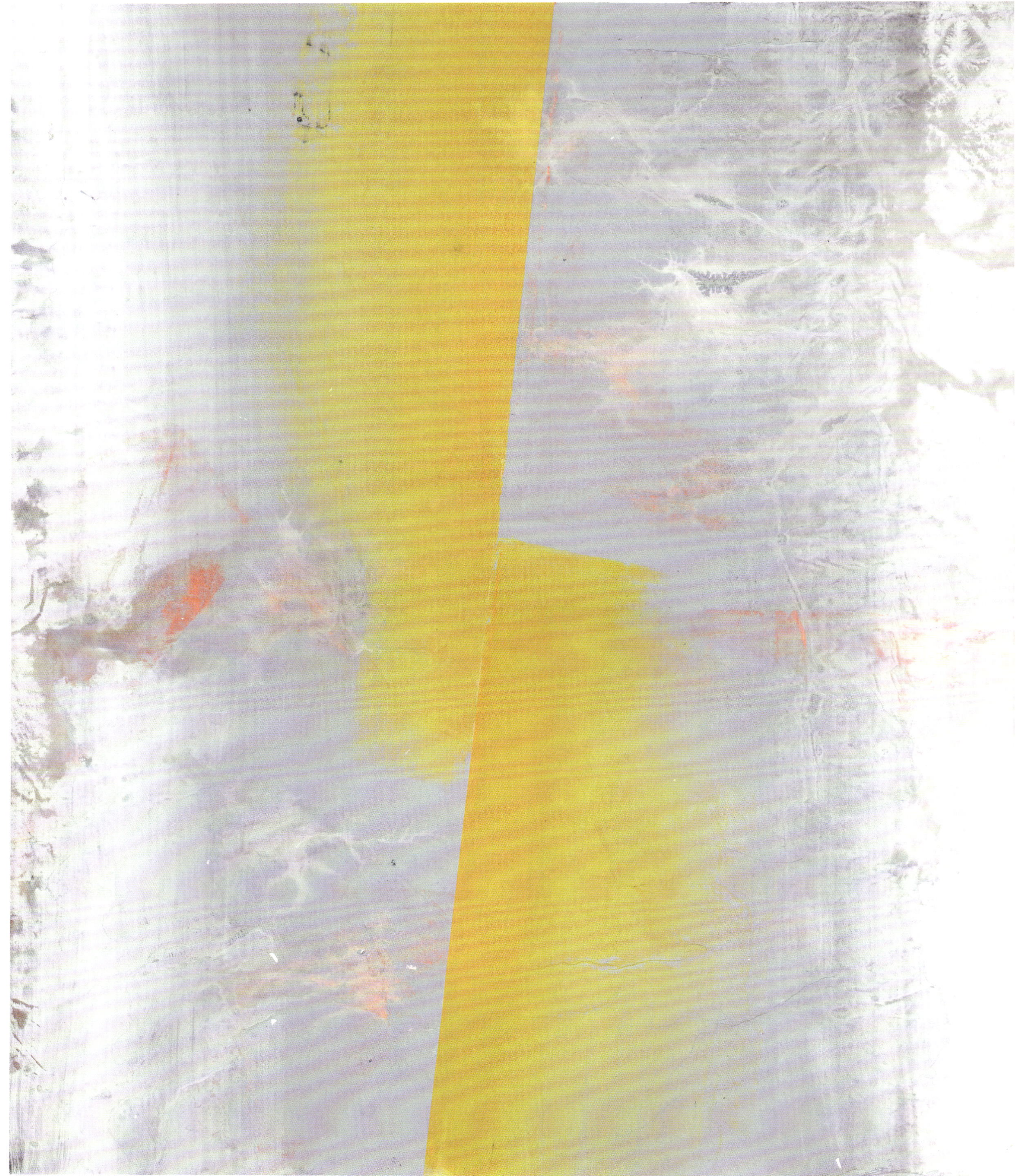

employing pigments can transform his repertoire, incorporating tonal juxtapositions, saturations, and their interplay to conjure illusions of space, shadows, and light.

In the spring of 2024, Zheng debuted his color paintings in a private Hong Kong art space, 149Ruyi (fig. 2). Predominantly monochromatic with infusions of vibrant pigments, these works reflect the bold and experimental spirit cultivated through printmaking. By integrating gradients, blurring effects, and tonal contrasts to further accentuate illusions of space and light, Zheng seamlessly extended the techniques honed in his monotypes to his painting practice. In his recent monumental painting *Golden State* (2024; p. 77), he masterfully infuses vibrant, warm hues of yellow and orange into the palette of his signature ink and acrylic painting. The result is a striking evolution: sculptural prisms that redefine and elevate his visual language, introducing unprecedented depth and luminosity to his oeuvre. A defining nexus in his practice, the injection of color has sparked a whole new way of bringing spectral phenomena to his paintings.

In this fluid osmosis between mediums, each discipline enriches and expands the possibilities of the other. This galvanizing cross-pollination enables Zheng to continually refine his artistic lexicon across diverse forms, always in flux, embodying the impermanence of any one method. Frequently drawing inspiration from—and honoring the sovereignty of—the materials at hand, whether ink or paint, Zheng captures the ephemeral and the cosmic beauty of natural phenomena. His works configure influences across time, space, and medium, transcending all boundaries except those of human perception.

Notes

1. *Qiyun* is the perceived energy or overall spirit of the artwork. The element of qiyun, according to sixth-century Chinese art historian Xie He, is believed to be essential, the most consequential factor for traditional Chinese ink painting. Zheng's interpretation of qiyun, combined with the Western philosophy of phenomenology, is the realization of experience and perception for the viewer.

2. Zheng Chongbin, conversation with the author, October 30, 2024.

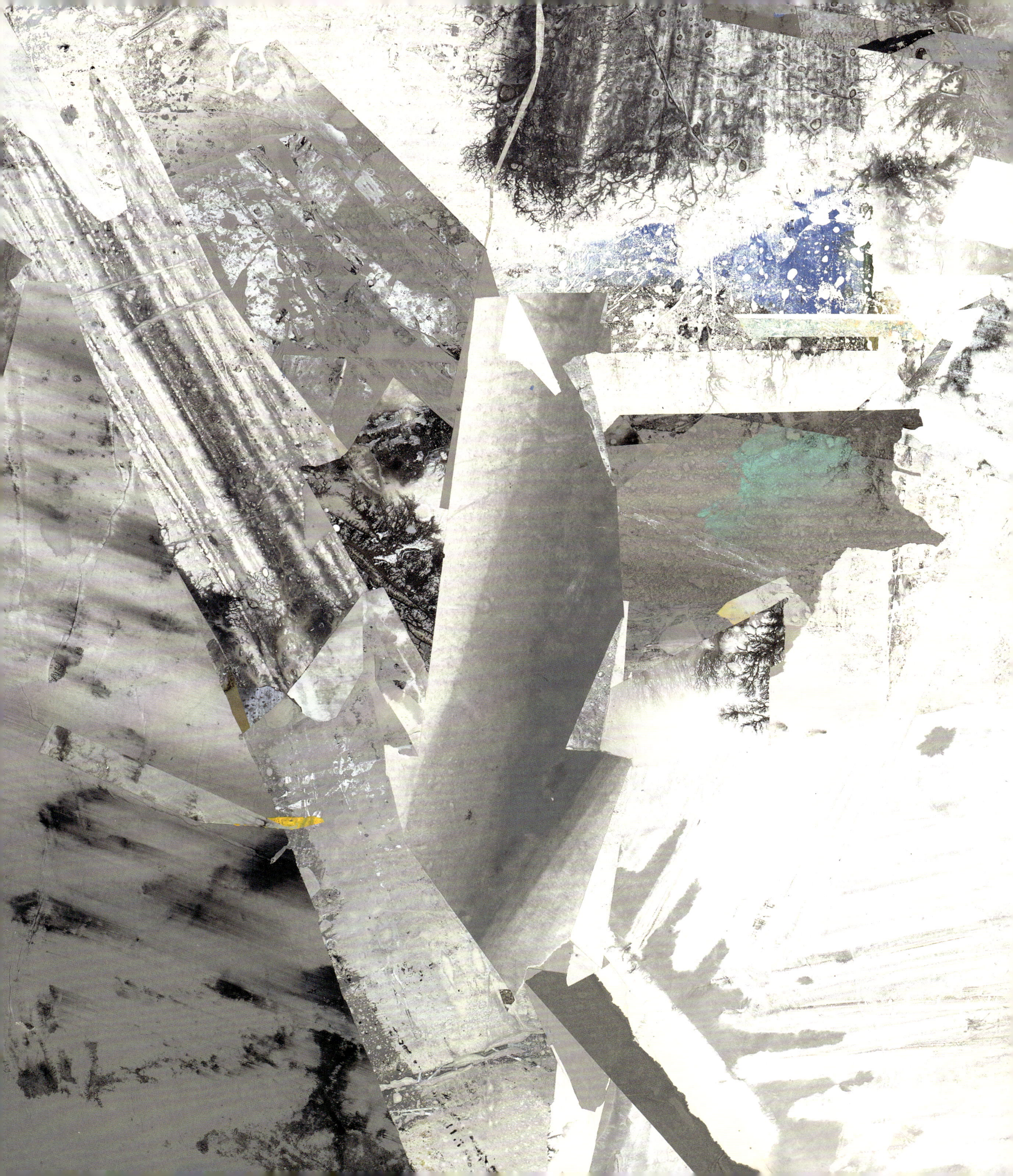

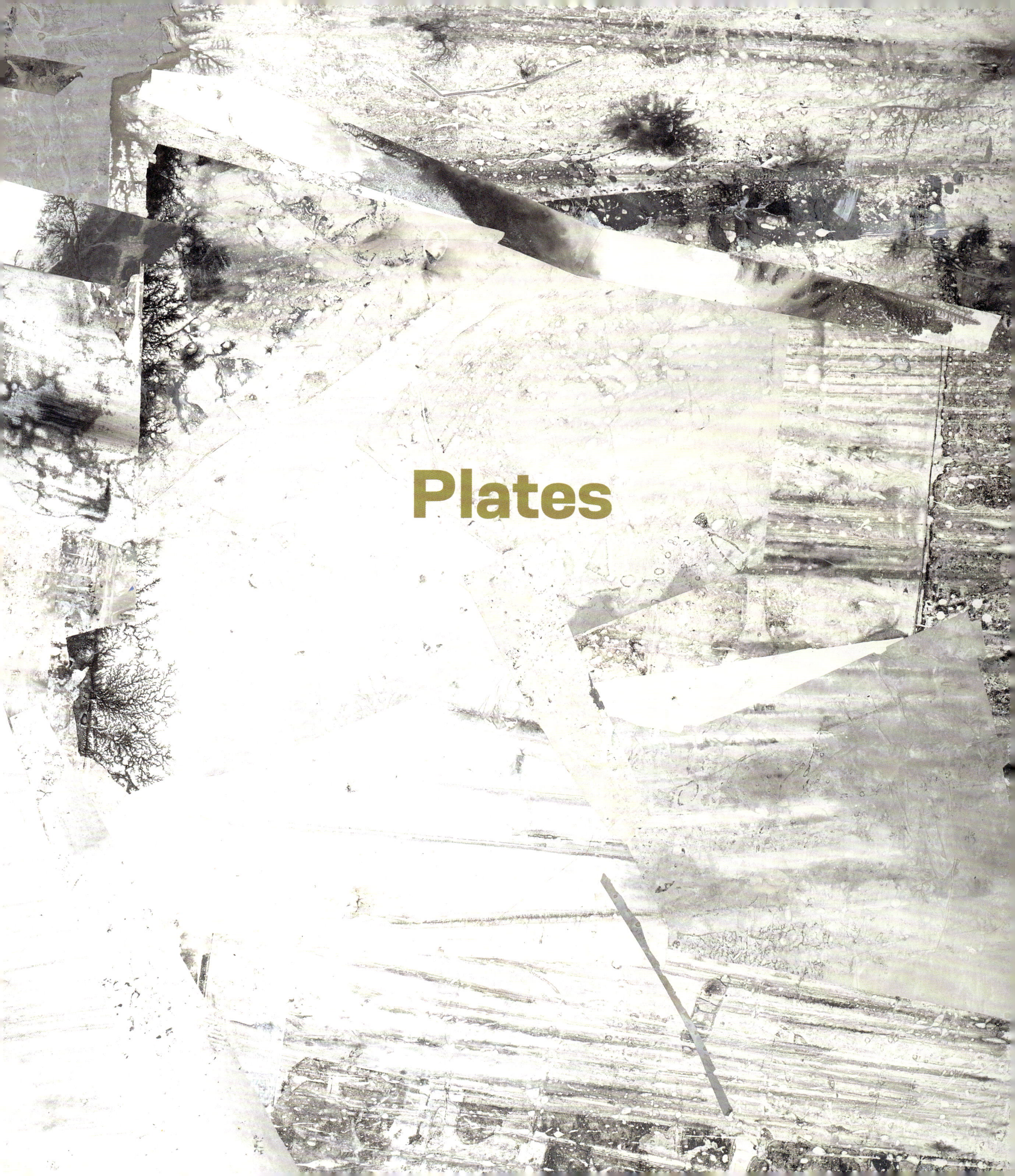

Plates

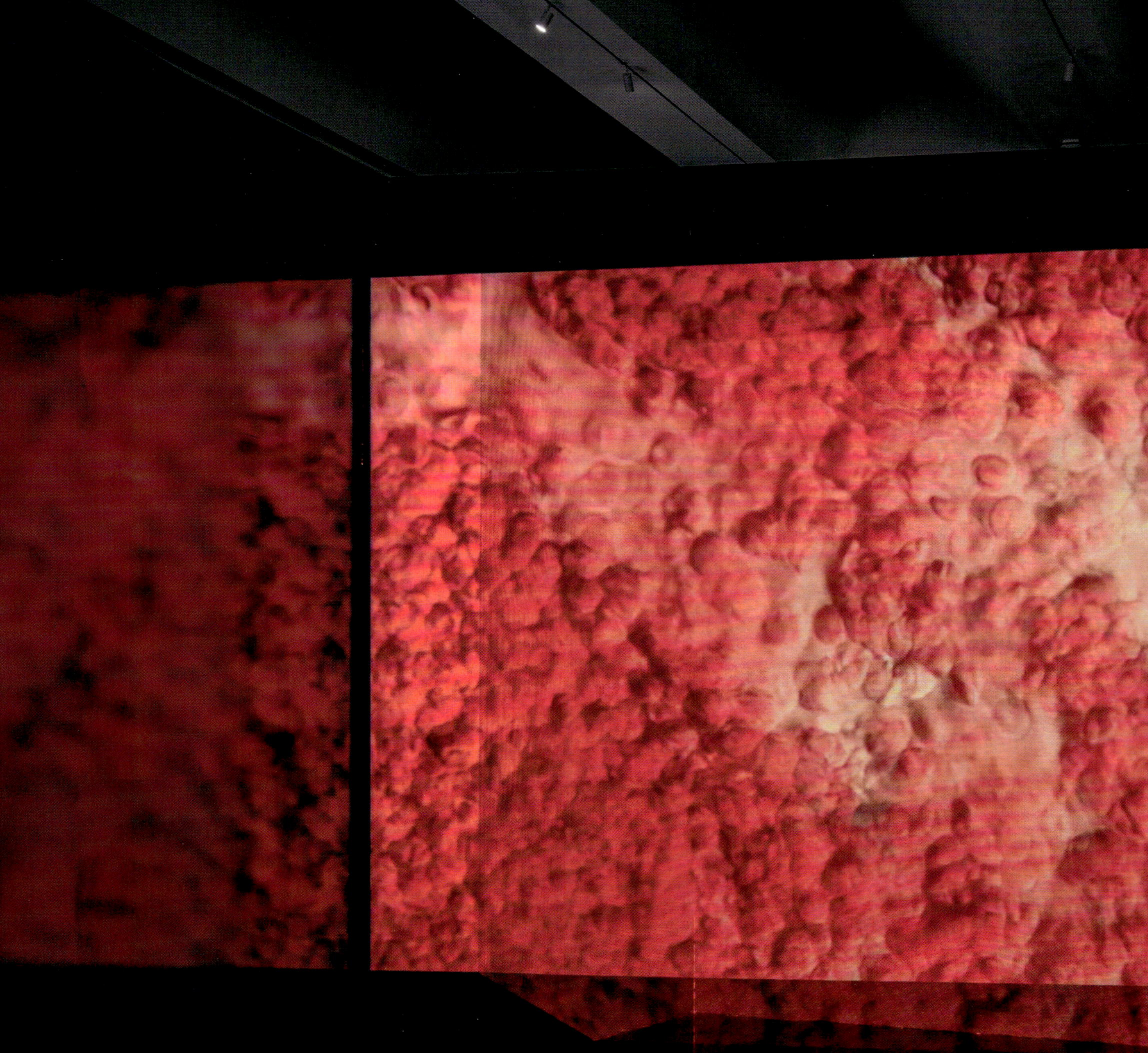

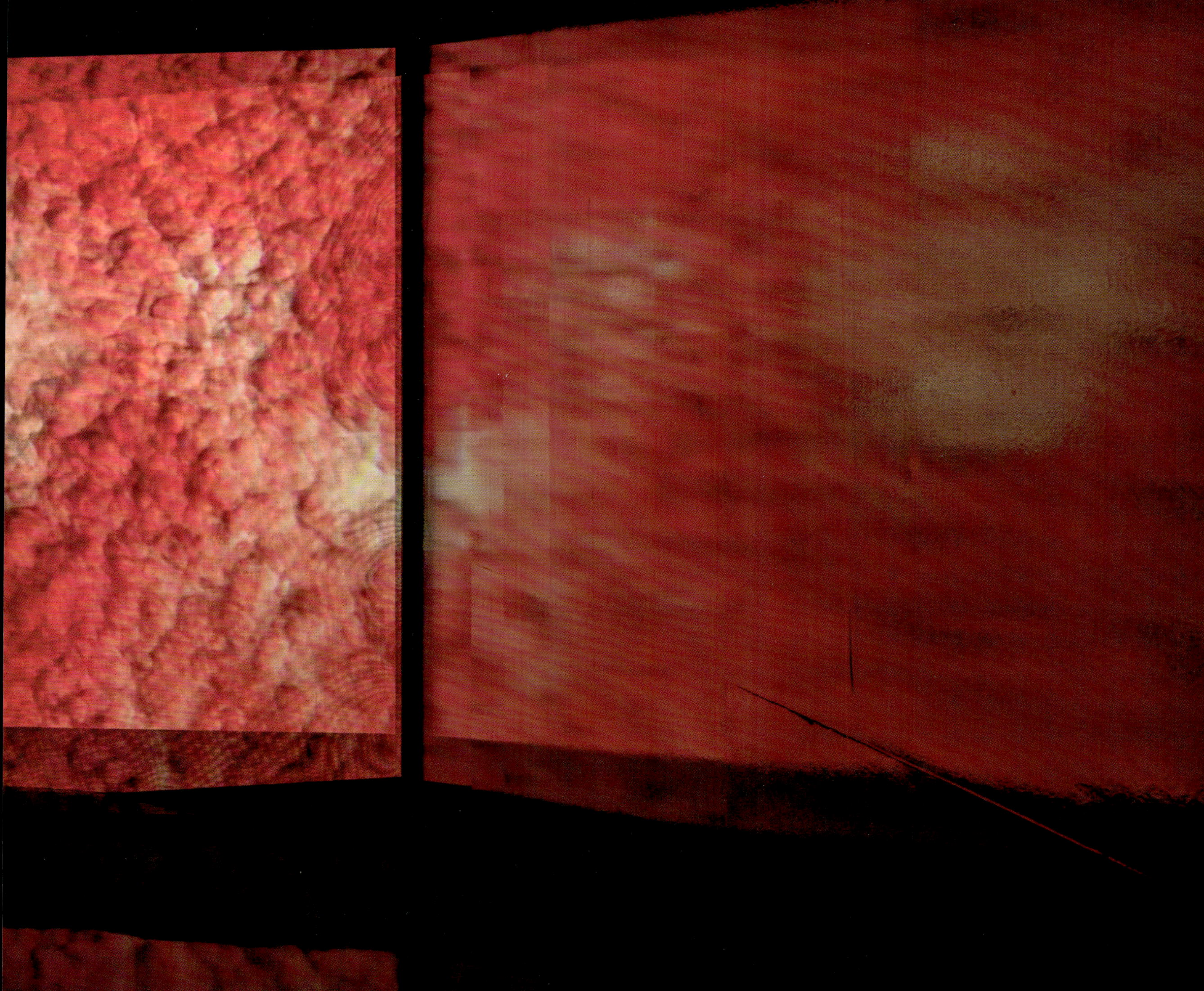

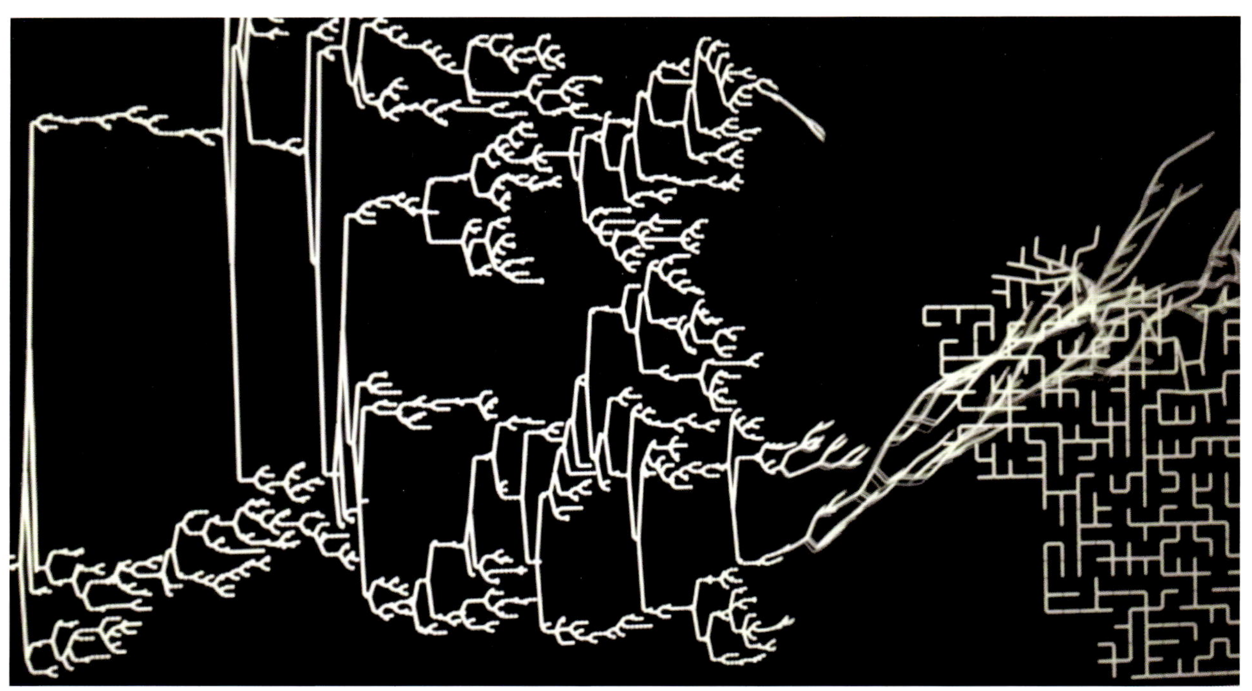

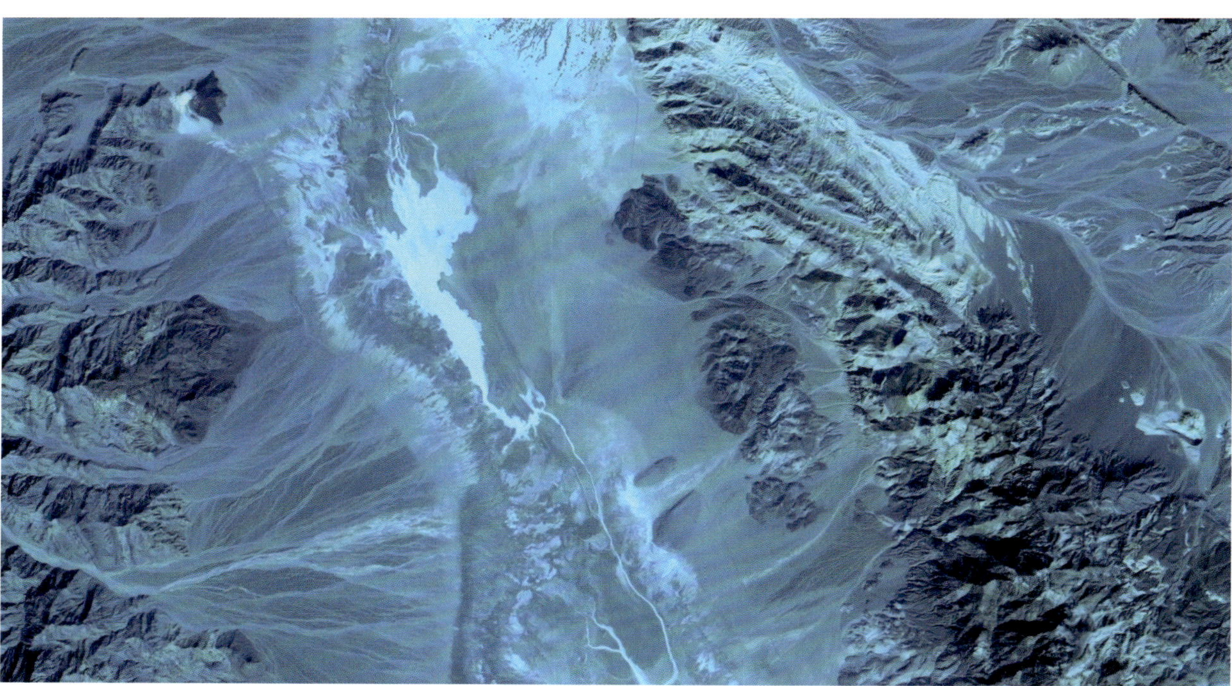

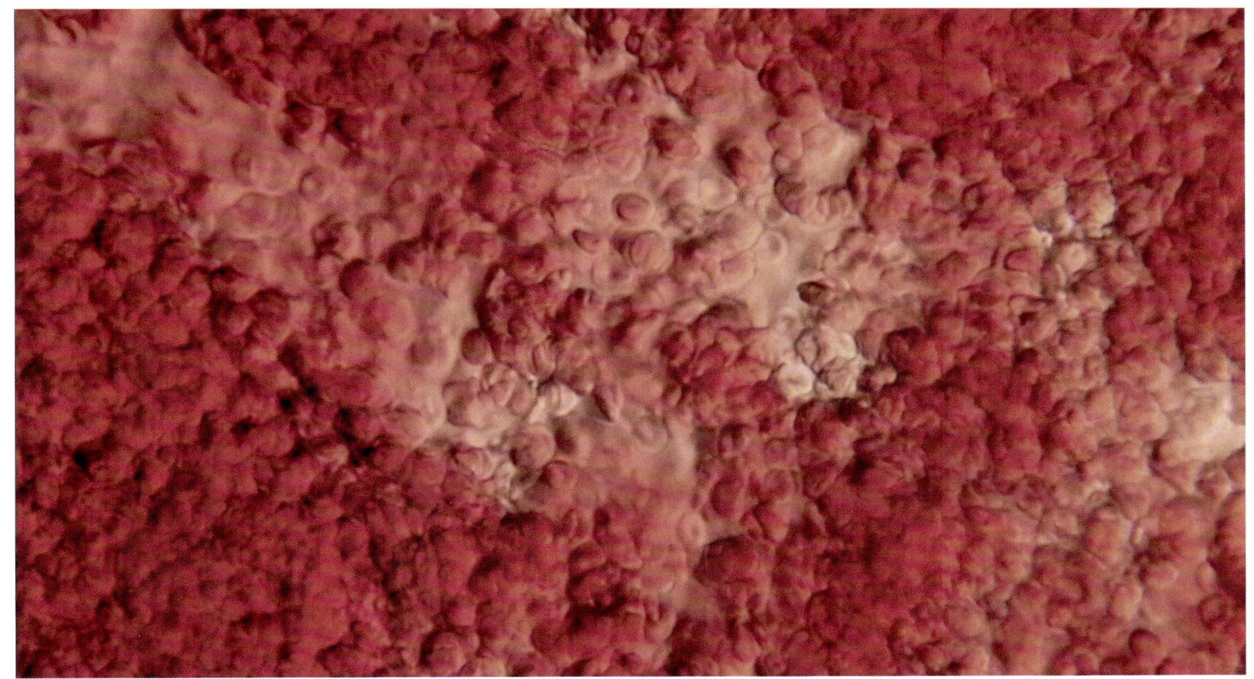

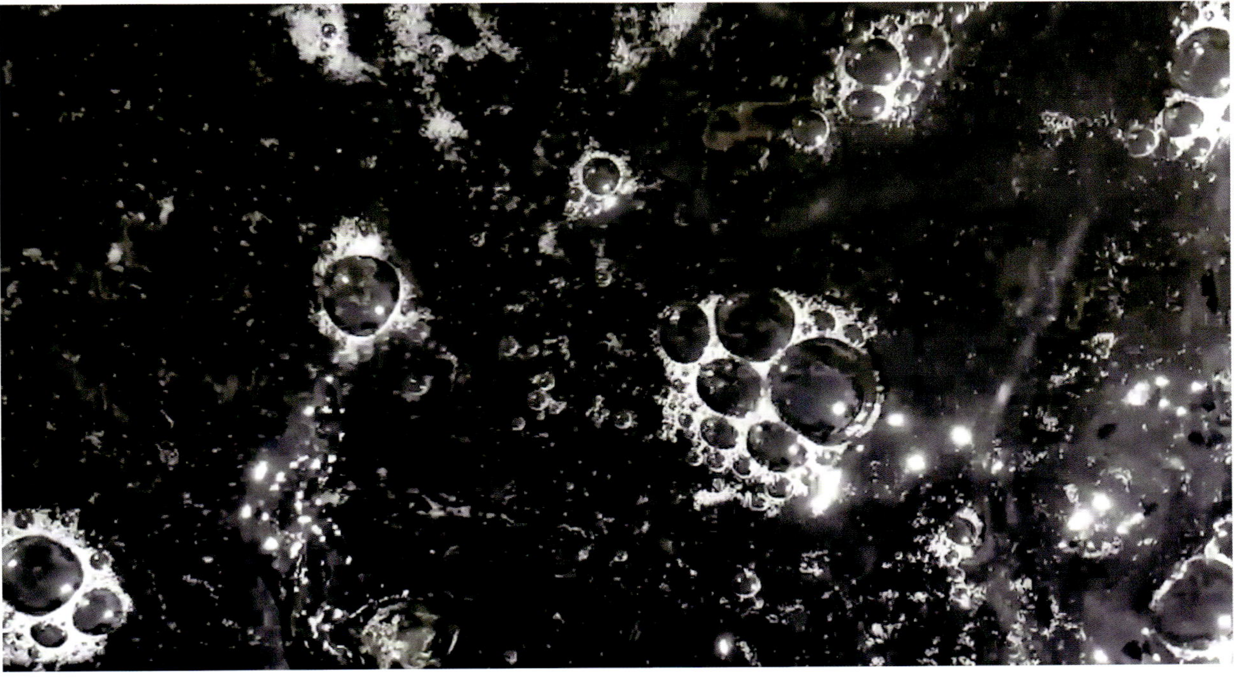

Chimeric Landscape, 2015
Video with color and sound on Betamax
cassette tape, wood frame, and scrim
Duration: 16 min., 50 sec.
Promised gift of the Fondation INK Collection

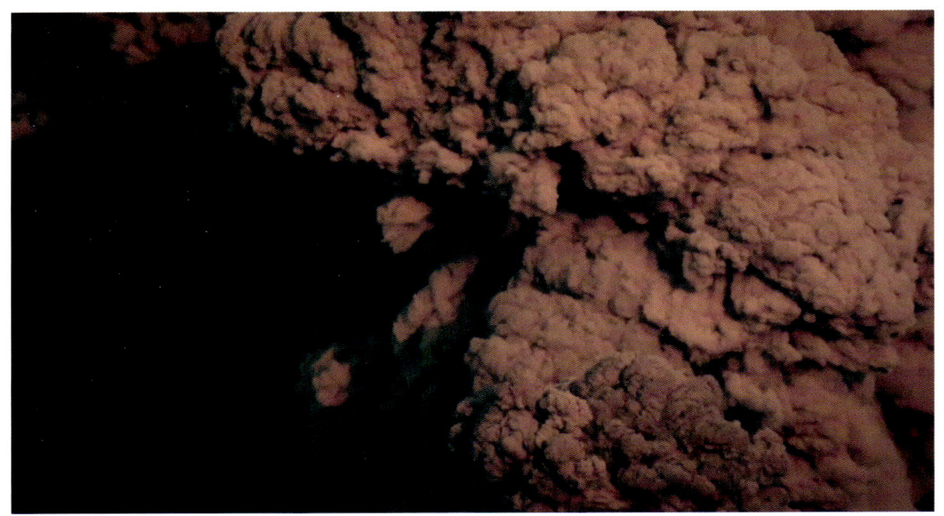

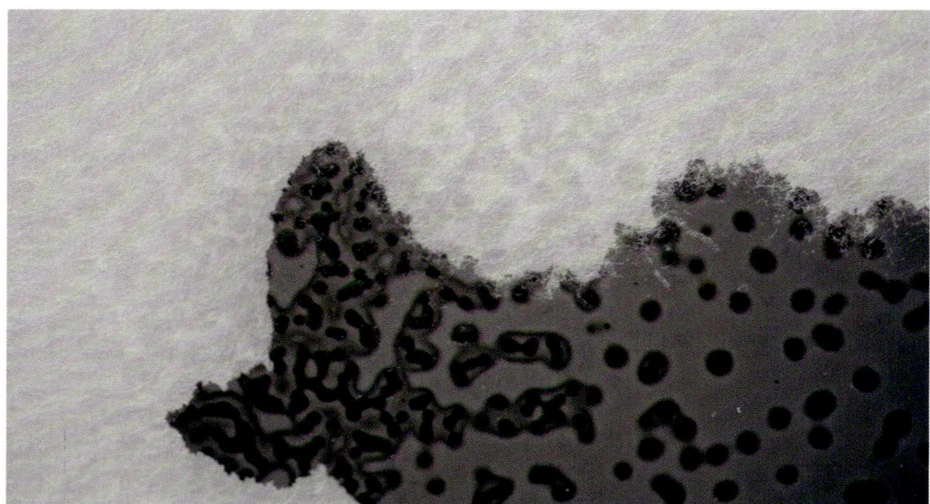

Chimeric Landscape, 2015
Video with color and sound on Betamax
cassette tape, wood frame, and scrim
Duration: 16 min., 50 sec.
Promised gift of the Fondation INK Collection

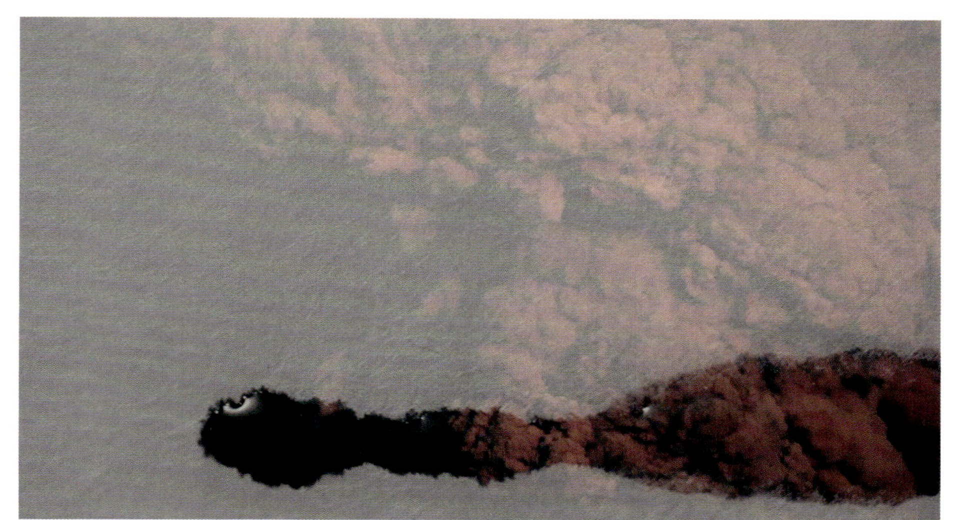

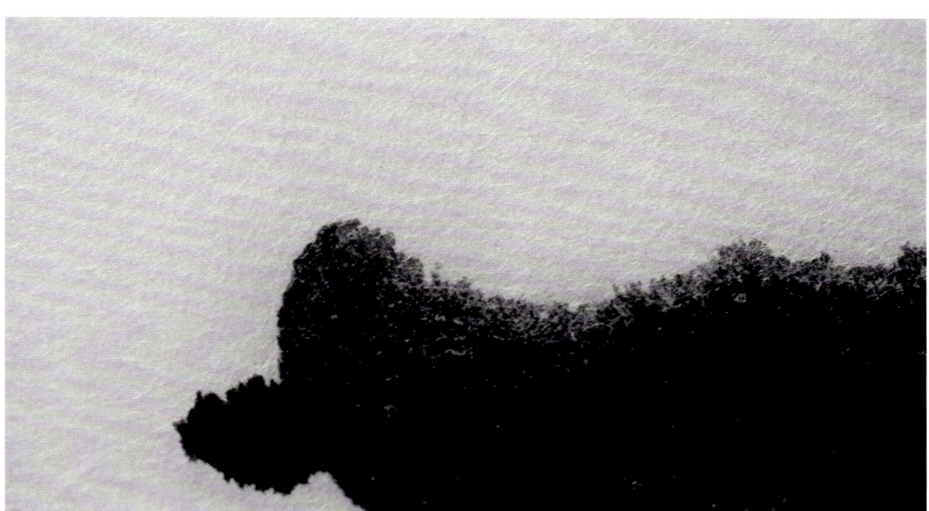

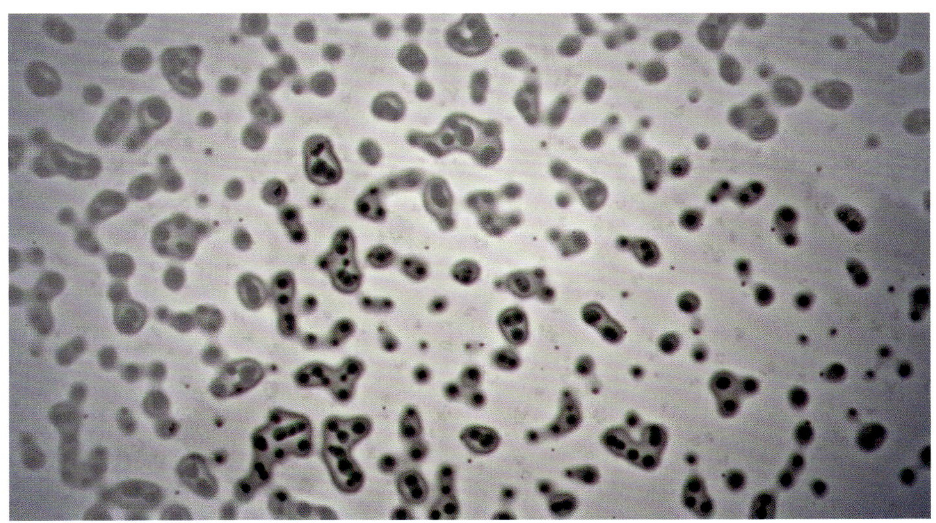

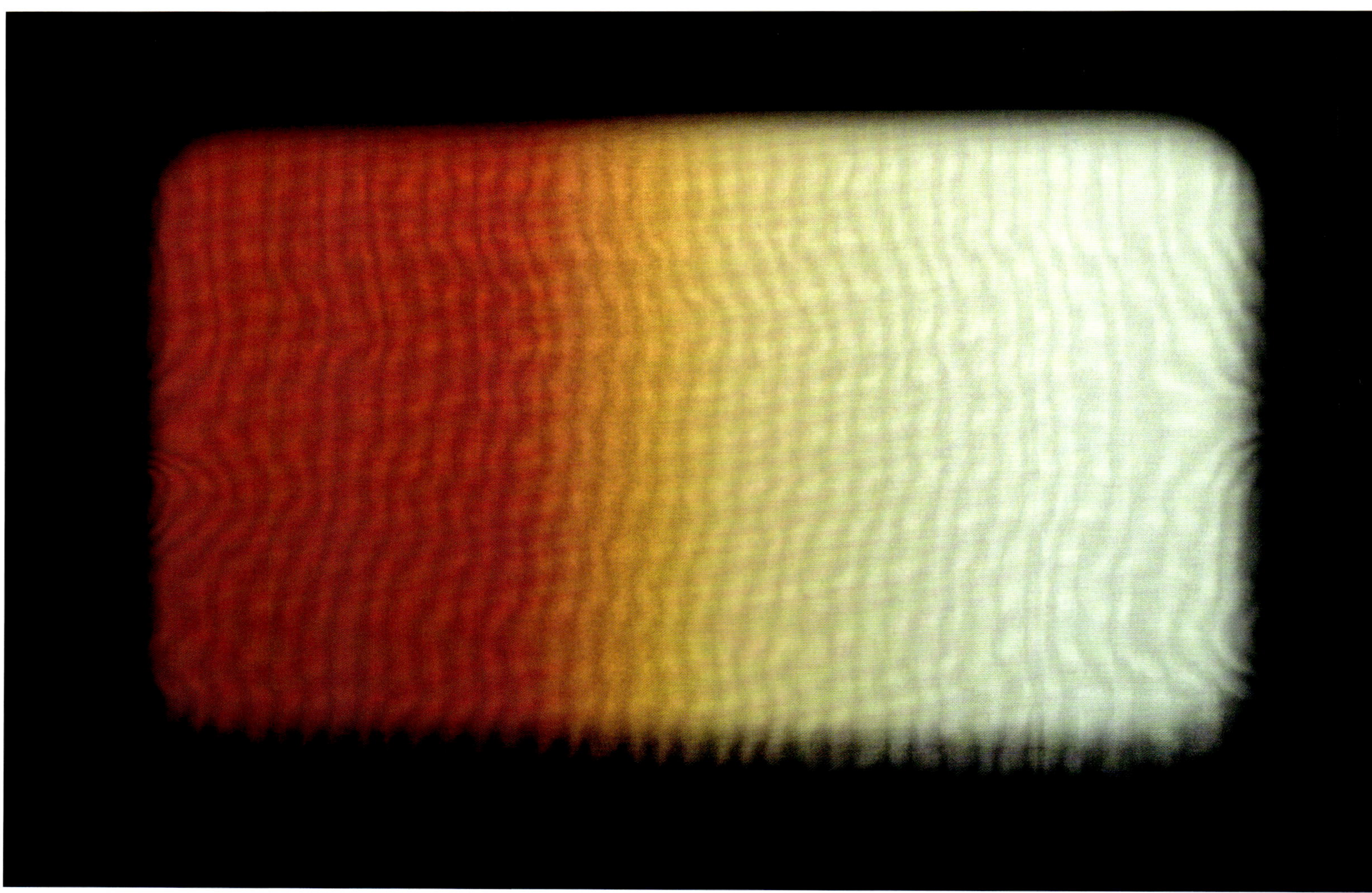

Mesh, 2018
Light-and-space installation with video projection,
wood frame, and scrim
Duration: 8 min., 35 sec.
LACMA

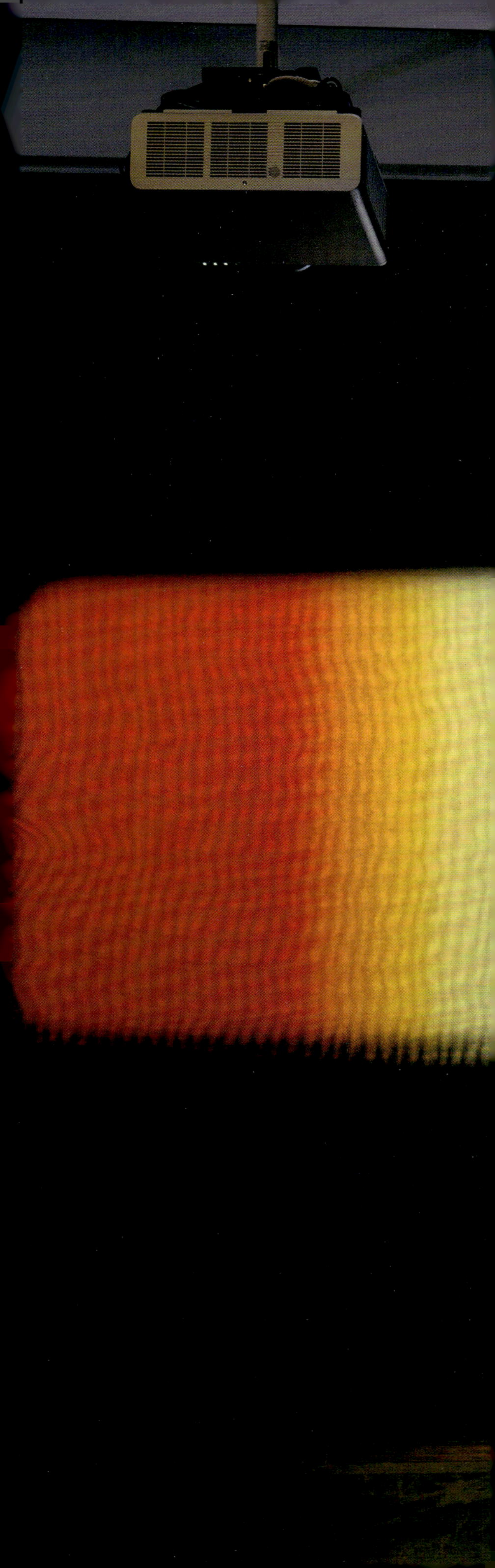

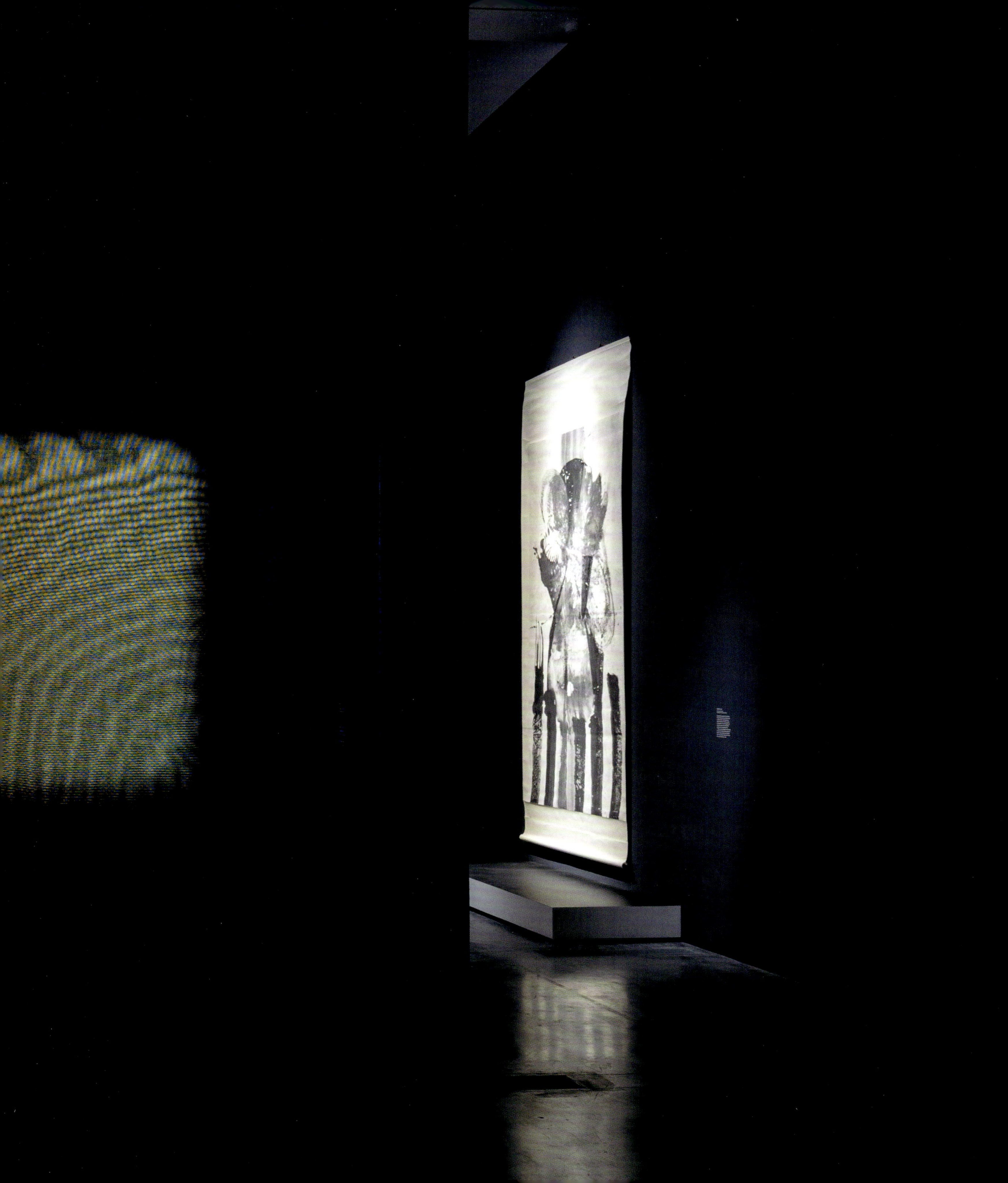

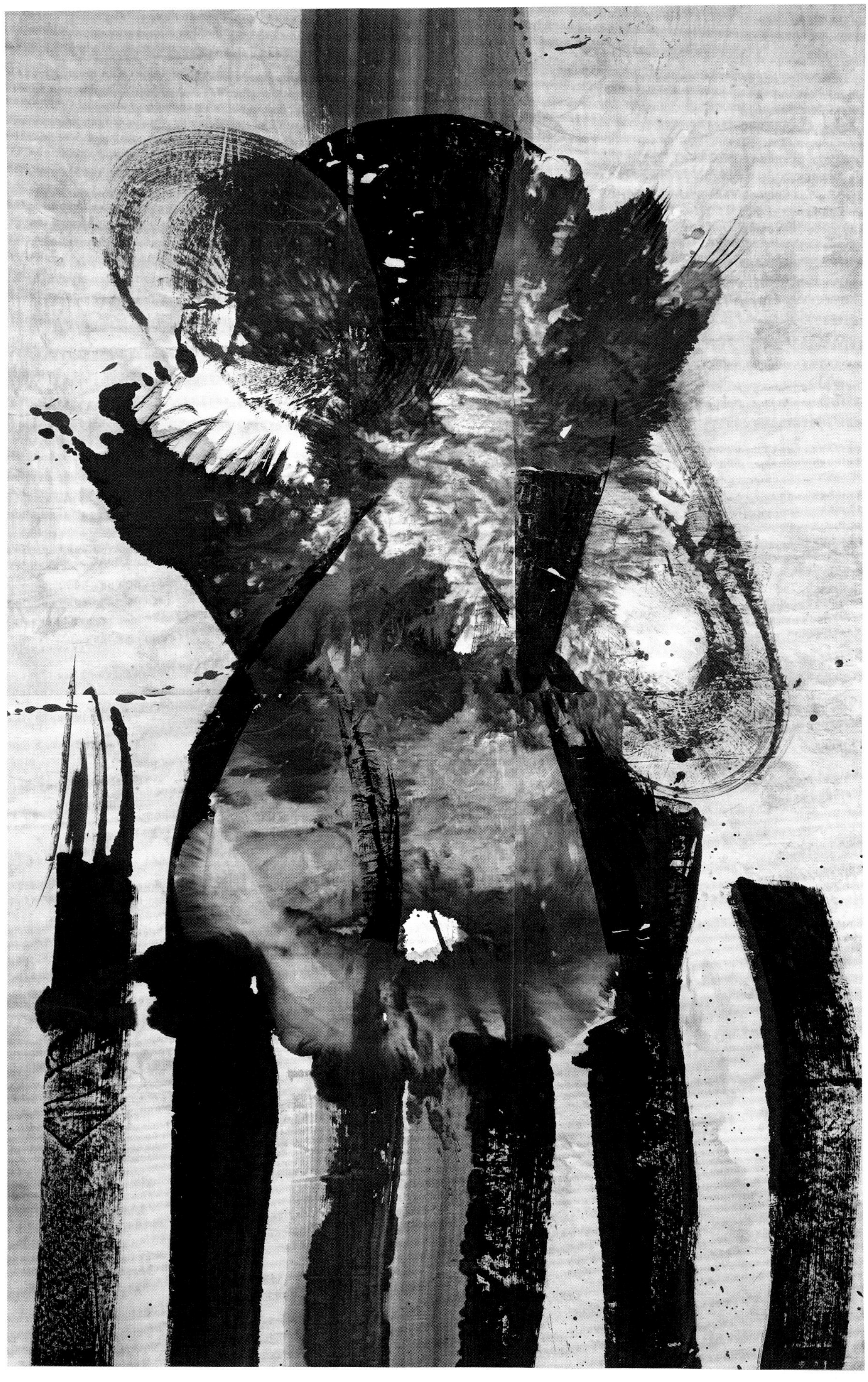

Untitled № 2, 1988
Ink and acrylic on xuan paper
136 × 70 in.
Promised gift of the Fondation INK Collection

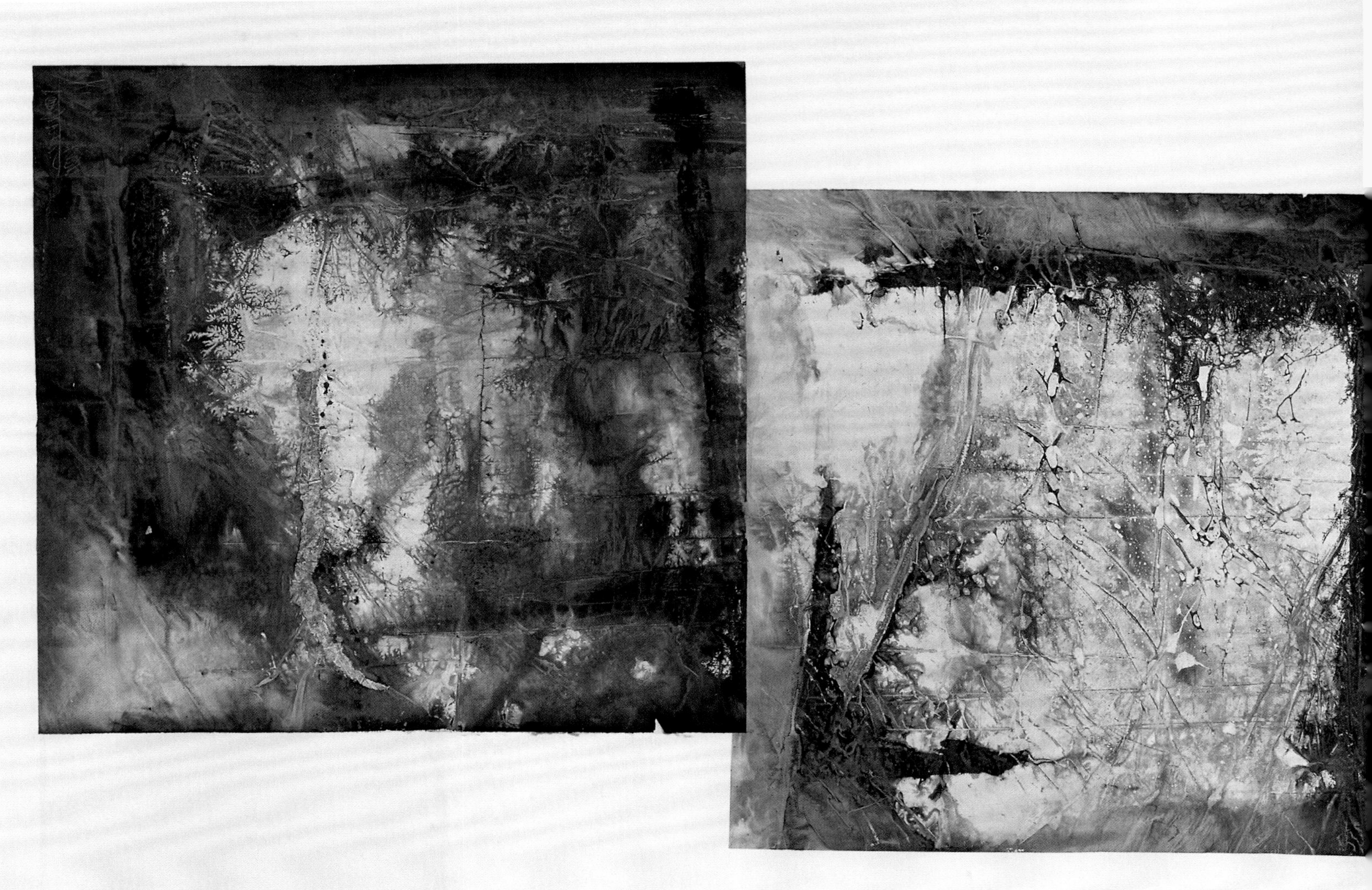

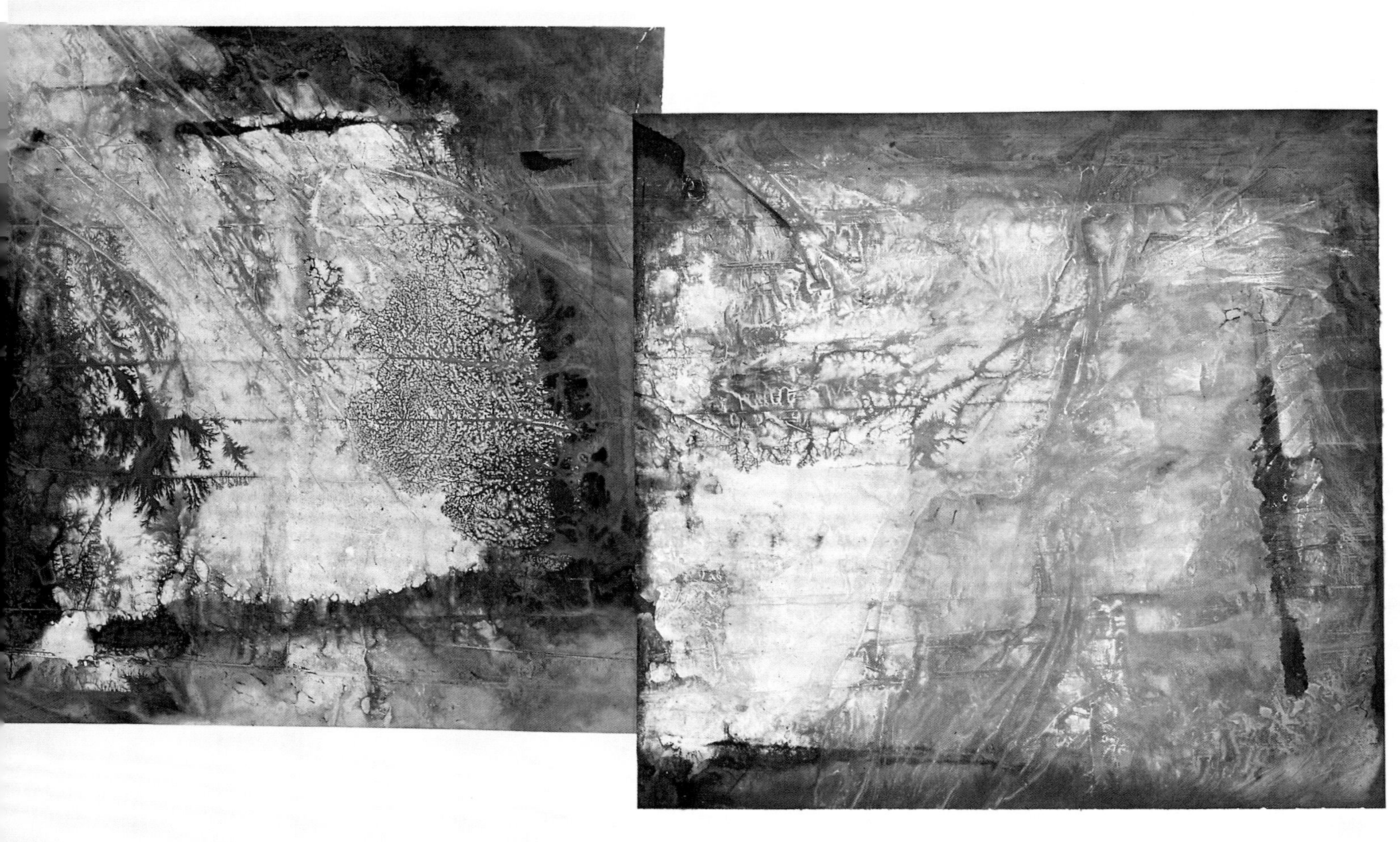

Four Overlap Atmospheres, 2012
Ink and acrylic on xuan paper
34⅜ × 98½ in.
Promised gift of the Fondation INK Collection

Turbulence, 2013
Ink and acrylic on xuan paper
125 × 71 × 2⅞ in.
Gift of Stephen O. Lesser

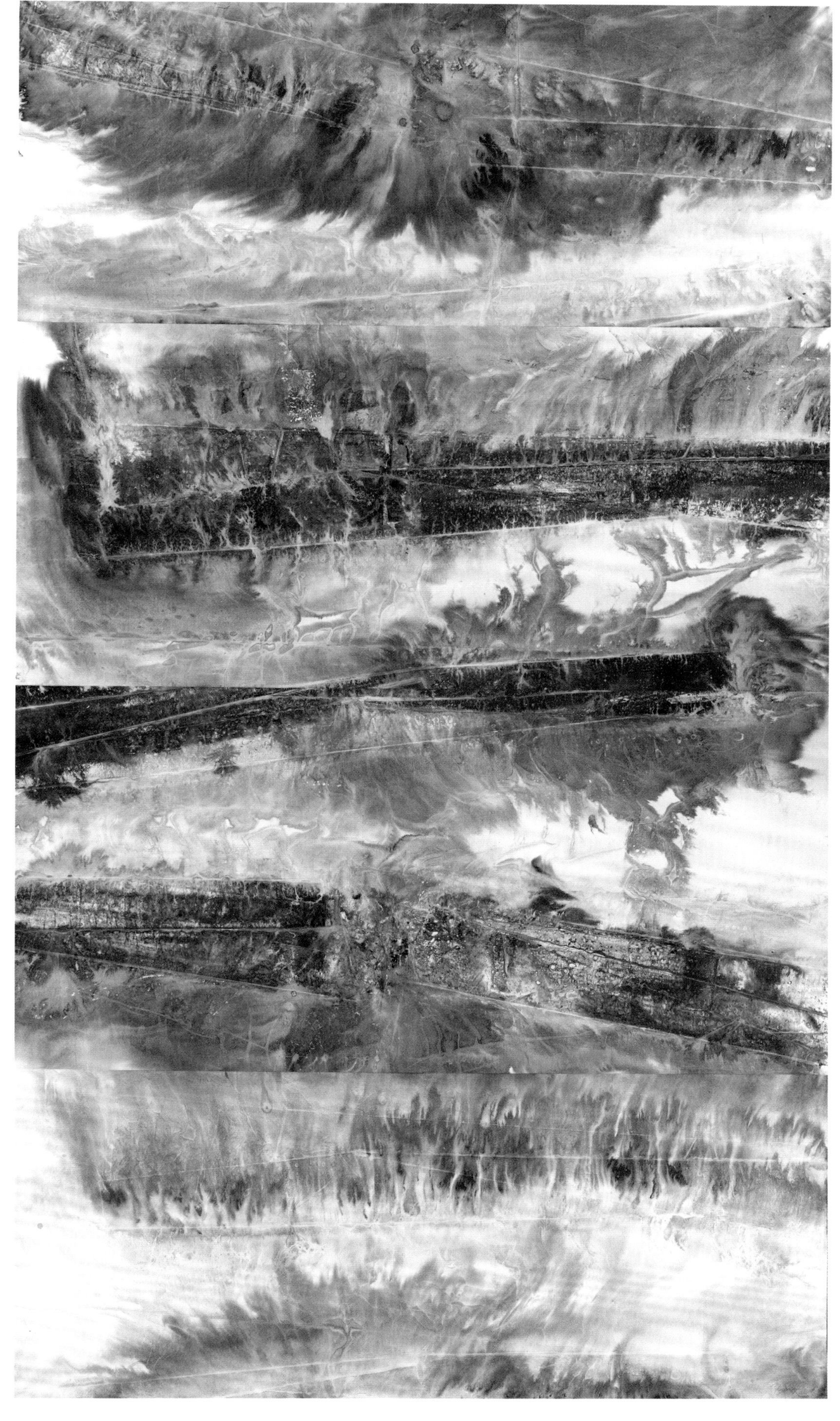

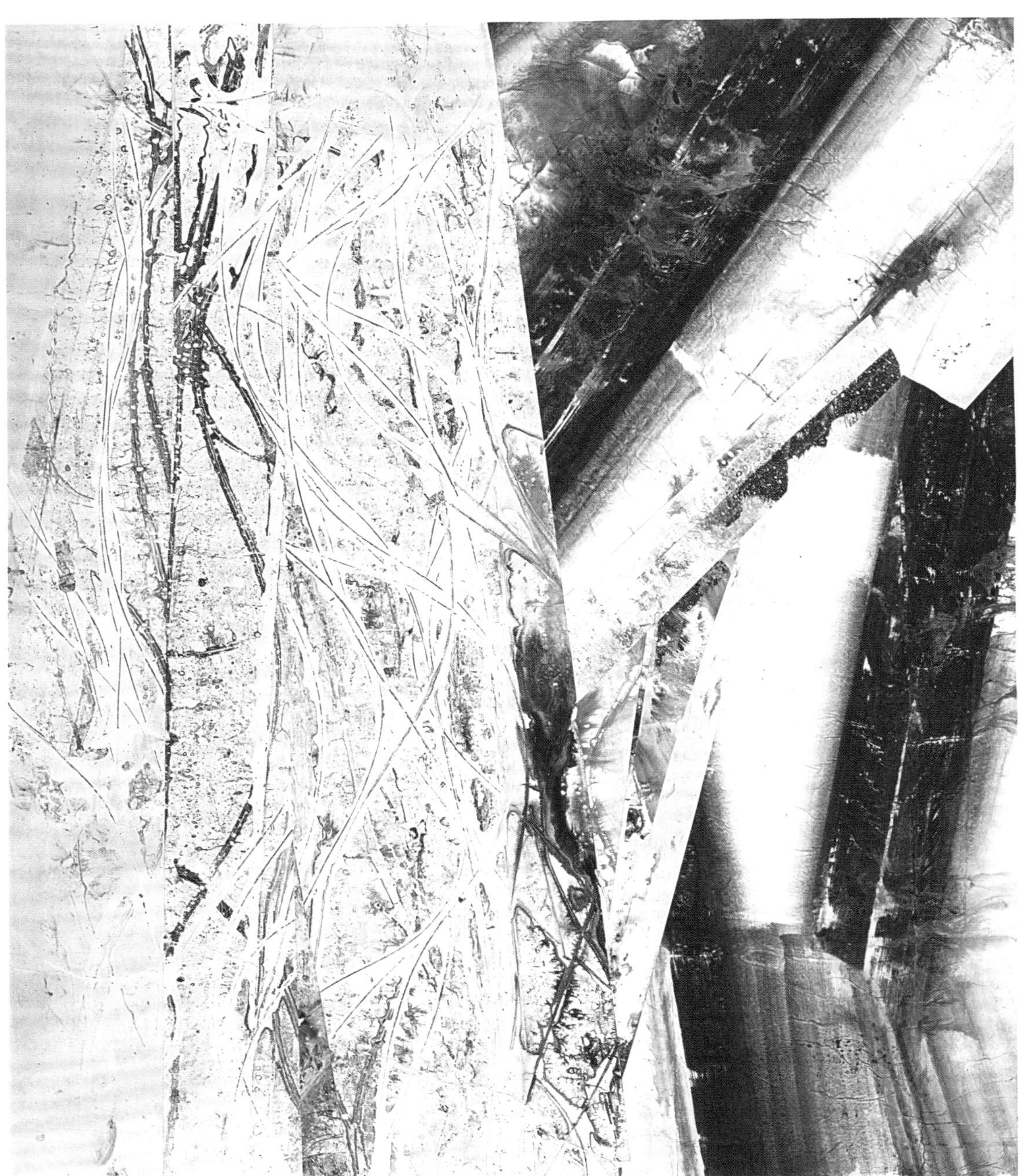

Between the Two Spaces, 2016
Ink and acrylic on xuan paper
77 × 65 in.
Jennifer and Mark McCormick

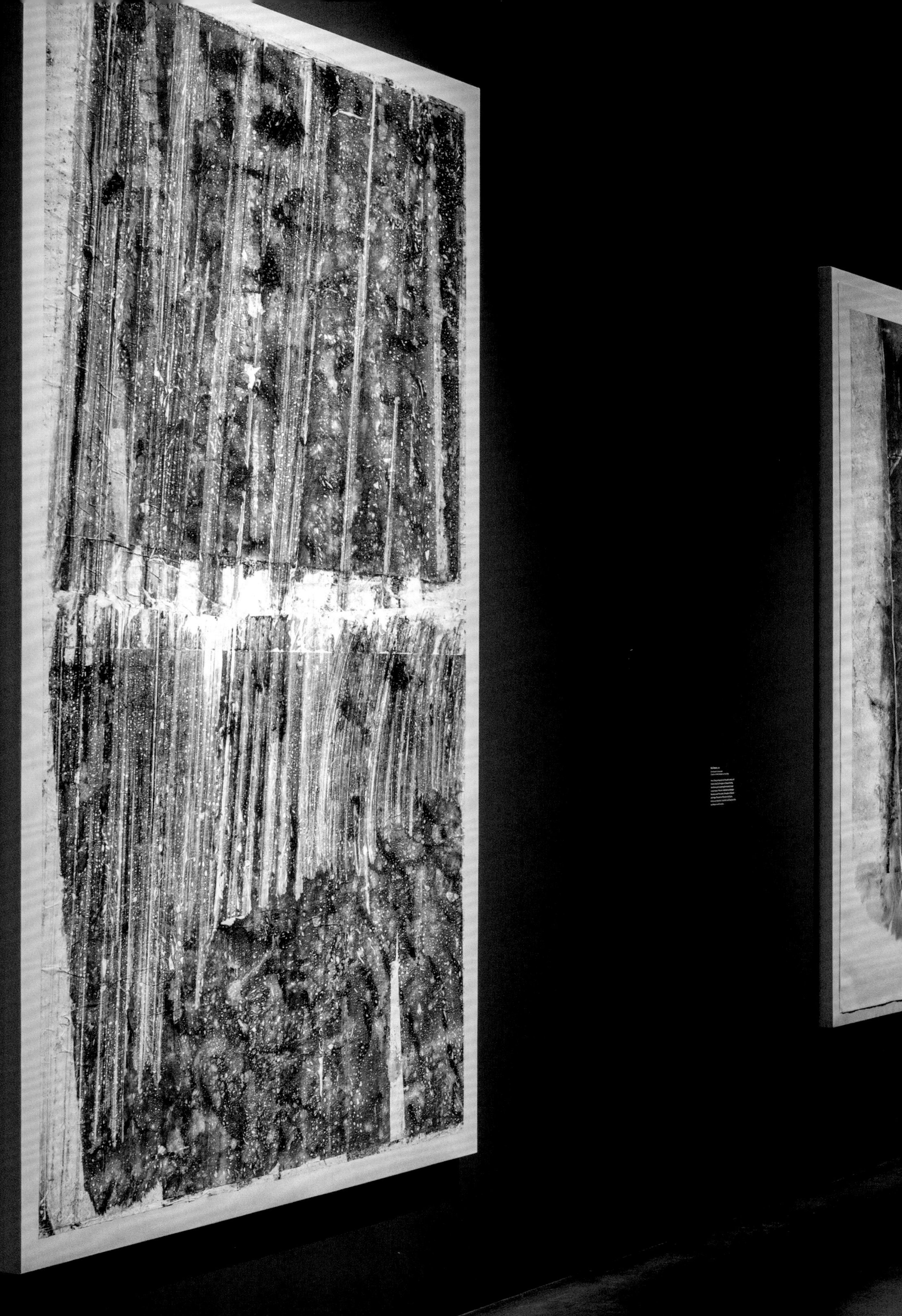

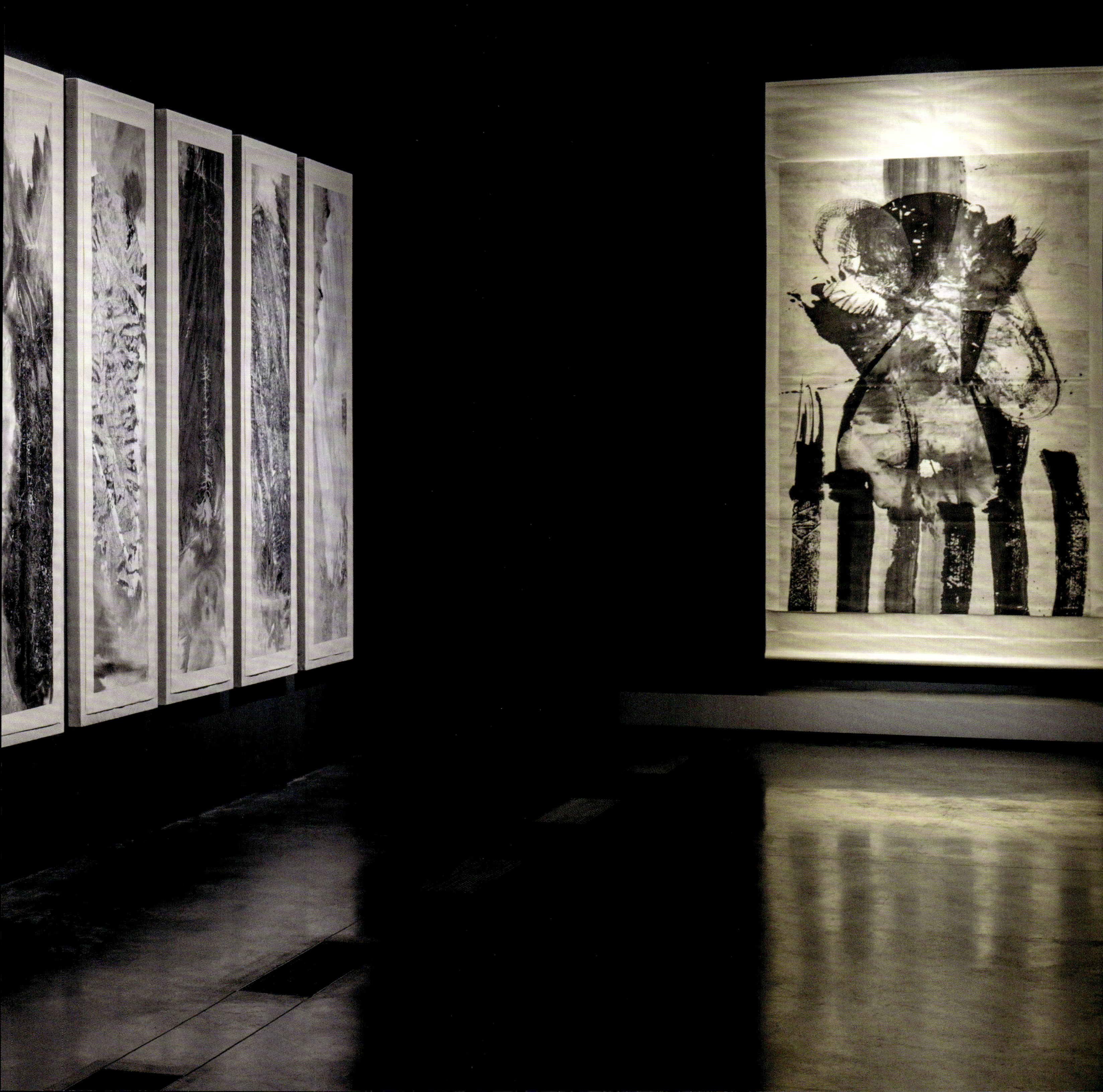

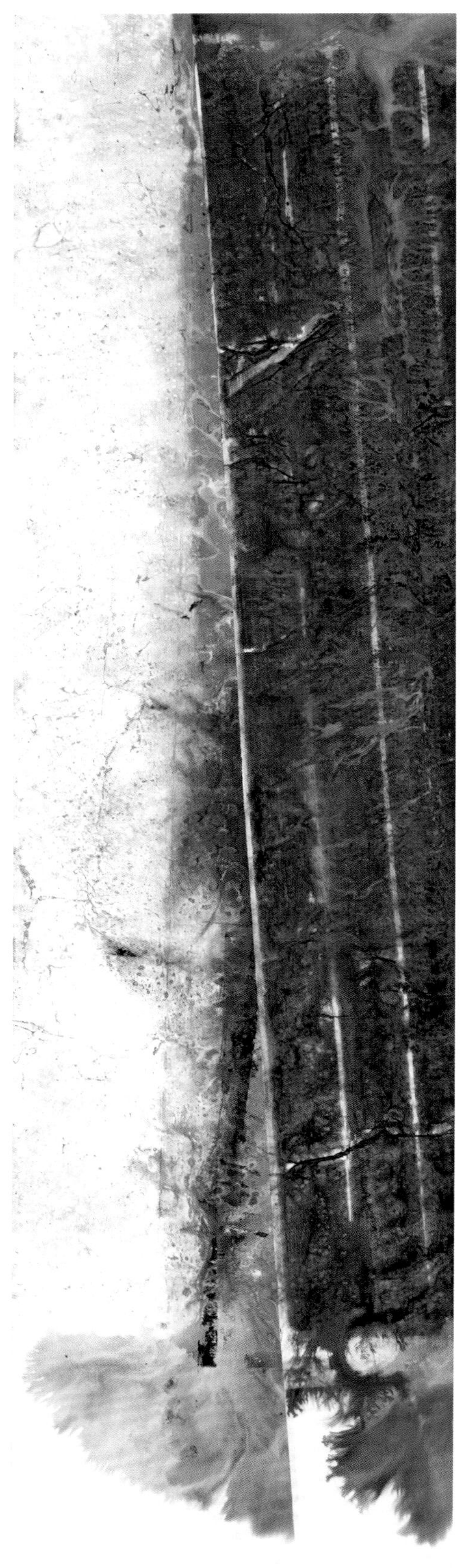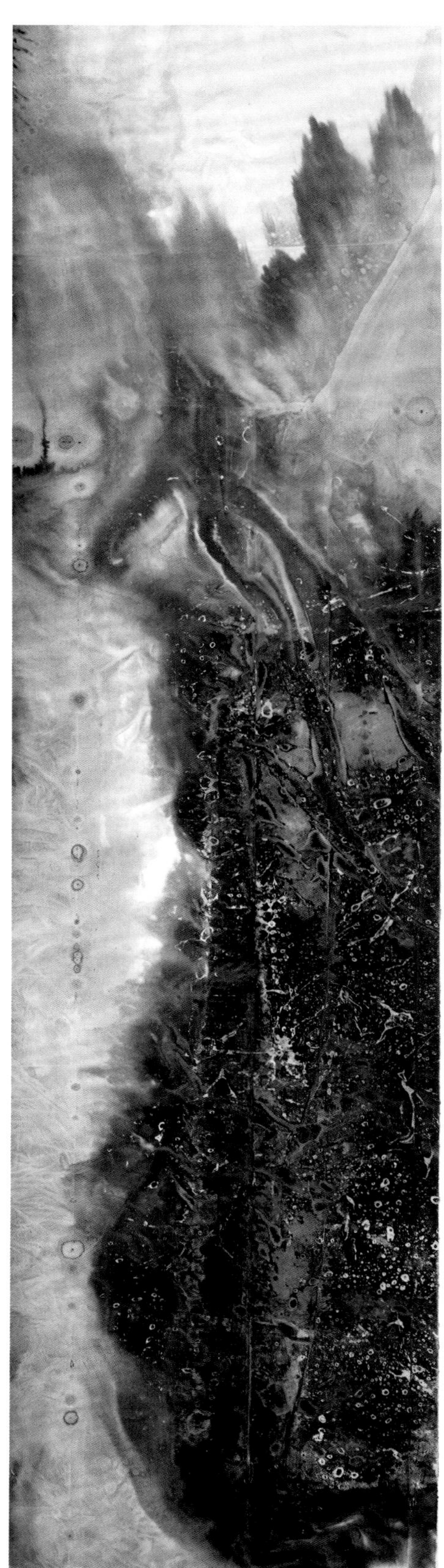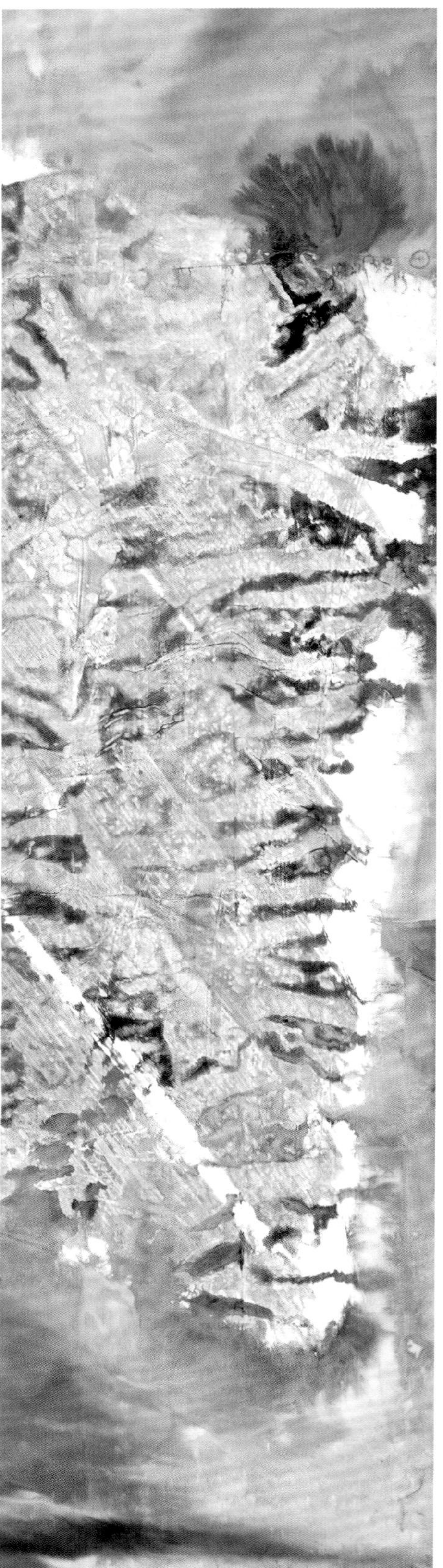

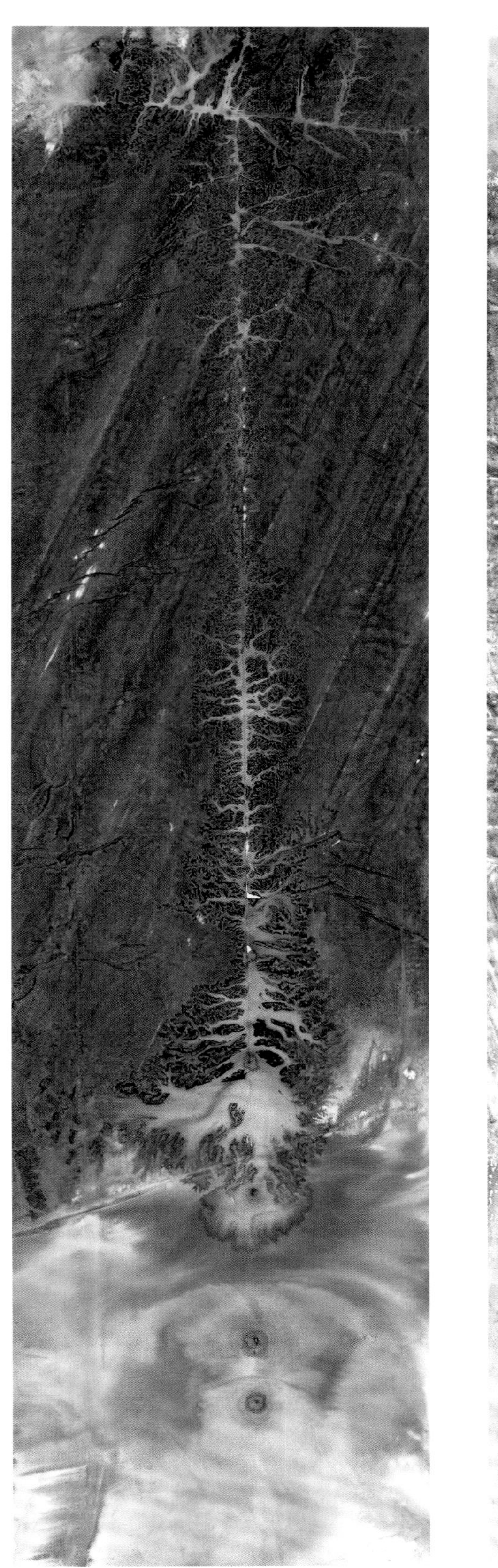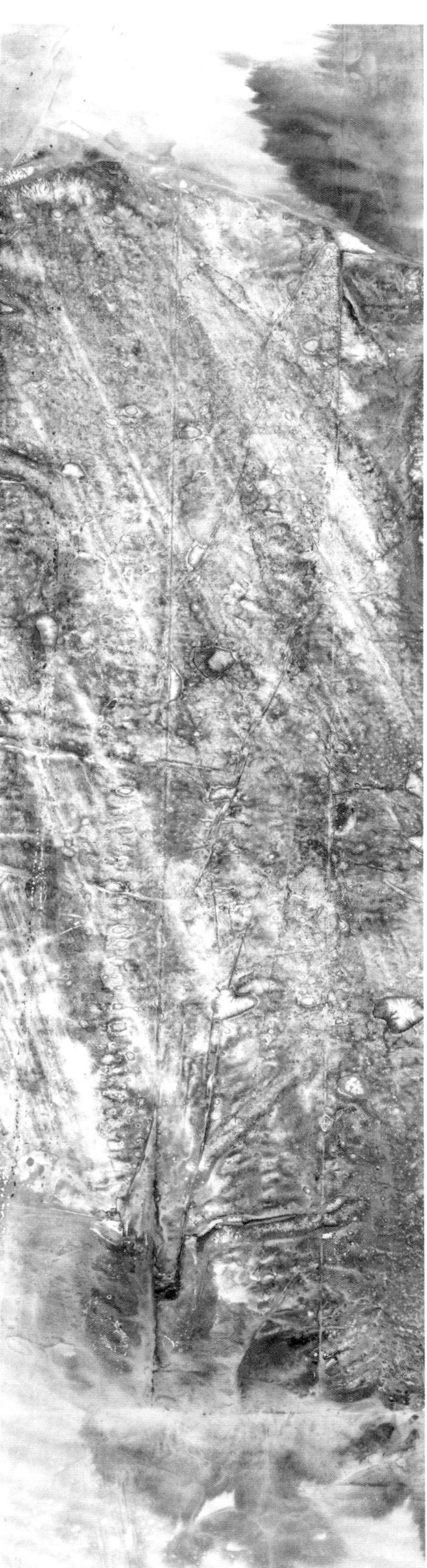

Six Canons, 2012
Ink and acrylic on xuan paper
Six panels, each 90½ × 24⅜ in.
Collection of Akiko Yamazaki and Jerry Yang

Trace, 2021
Ink and acrylic on xuan paper
109⅝ × 65 in.
Collection of the artist

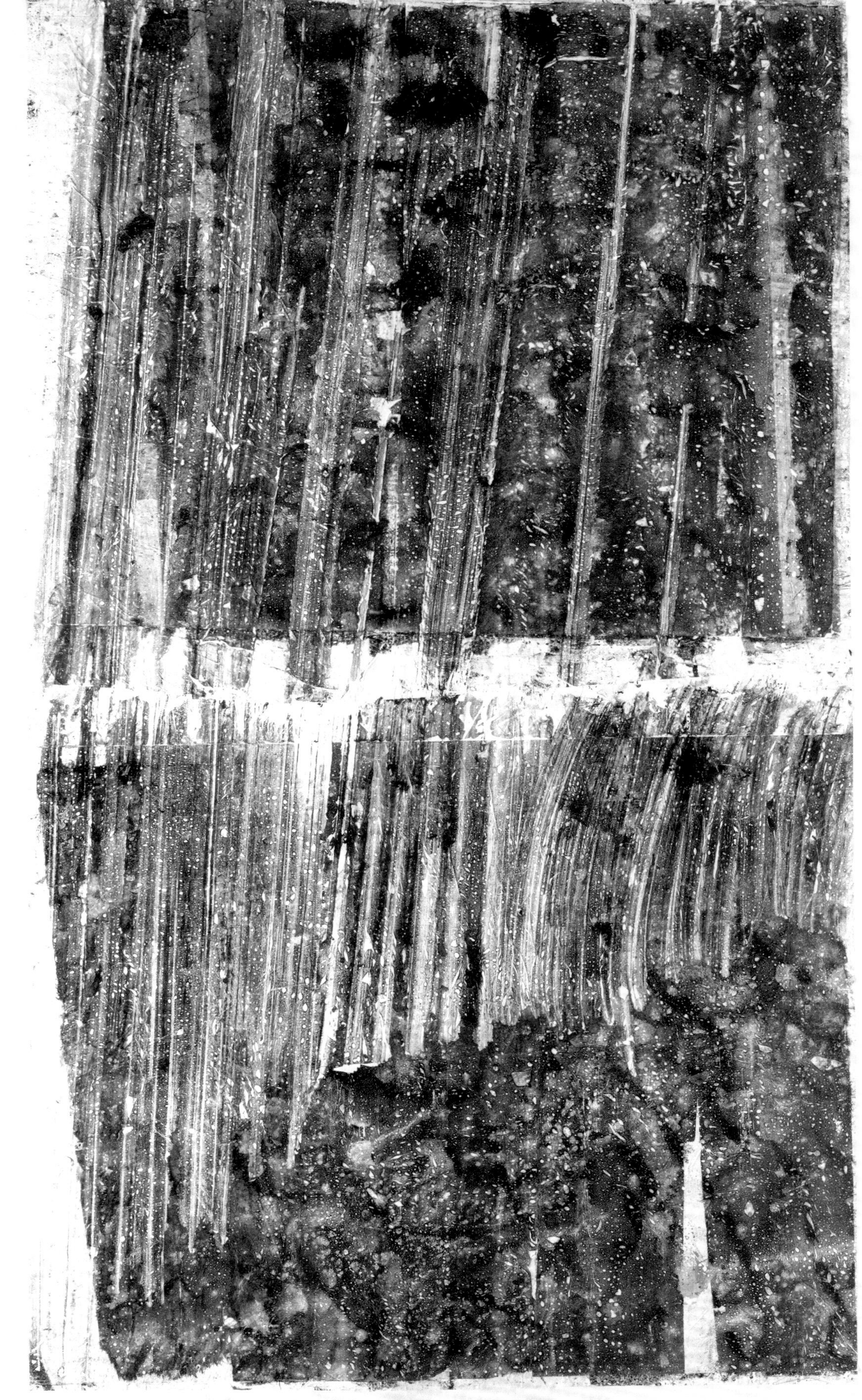

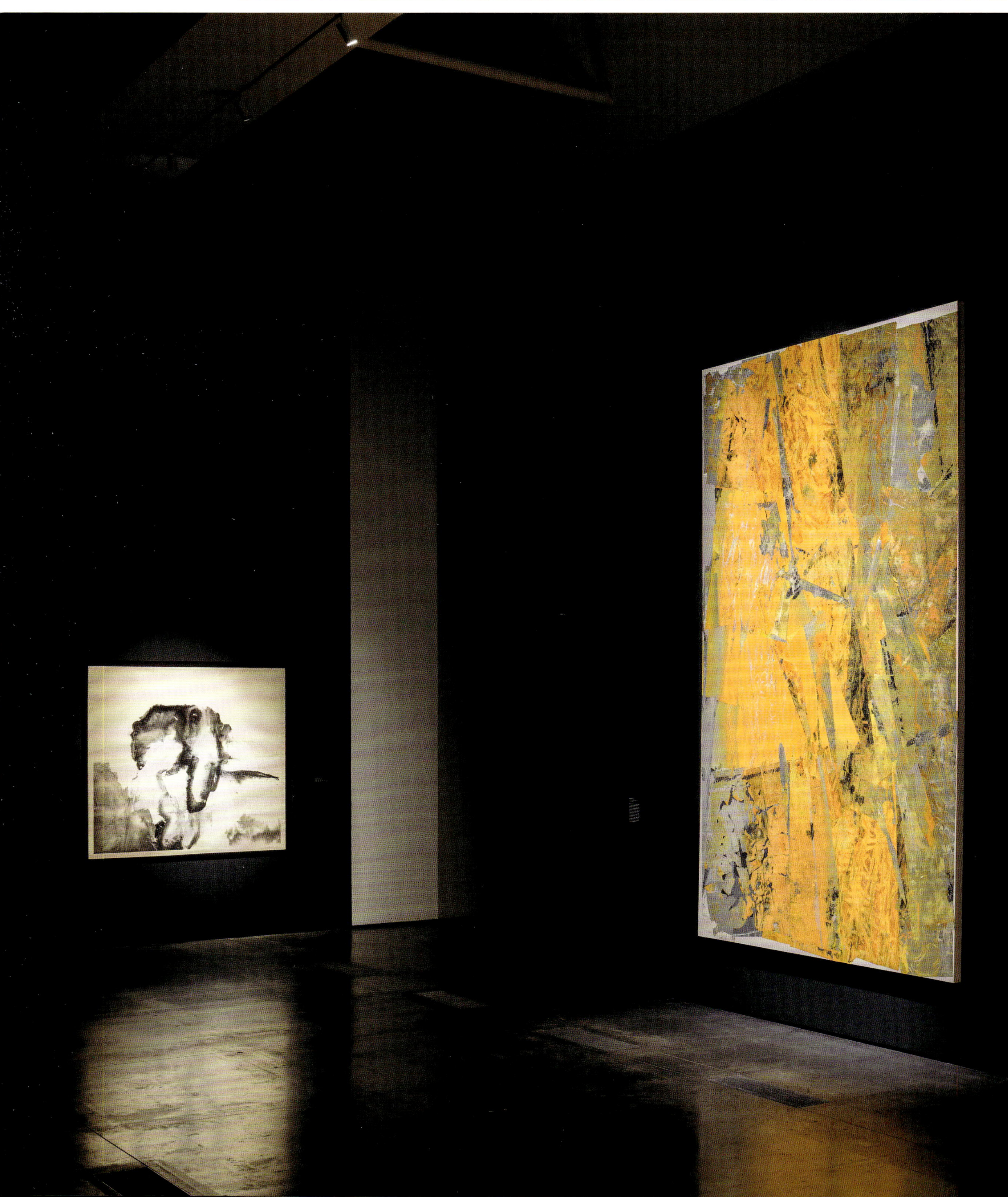

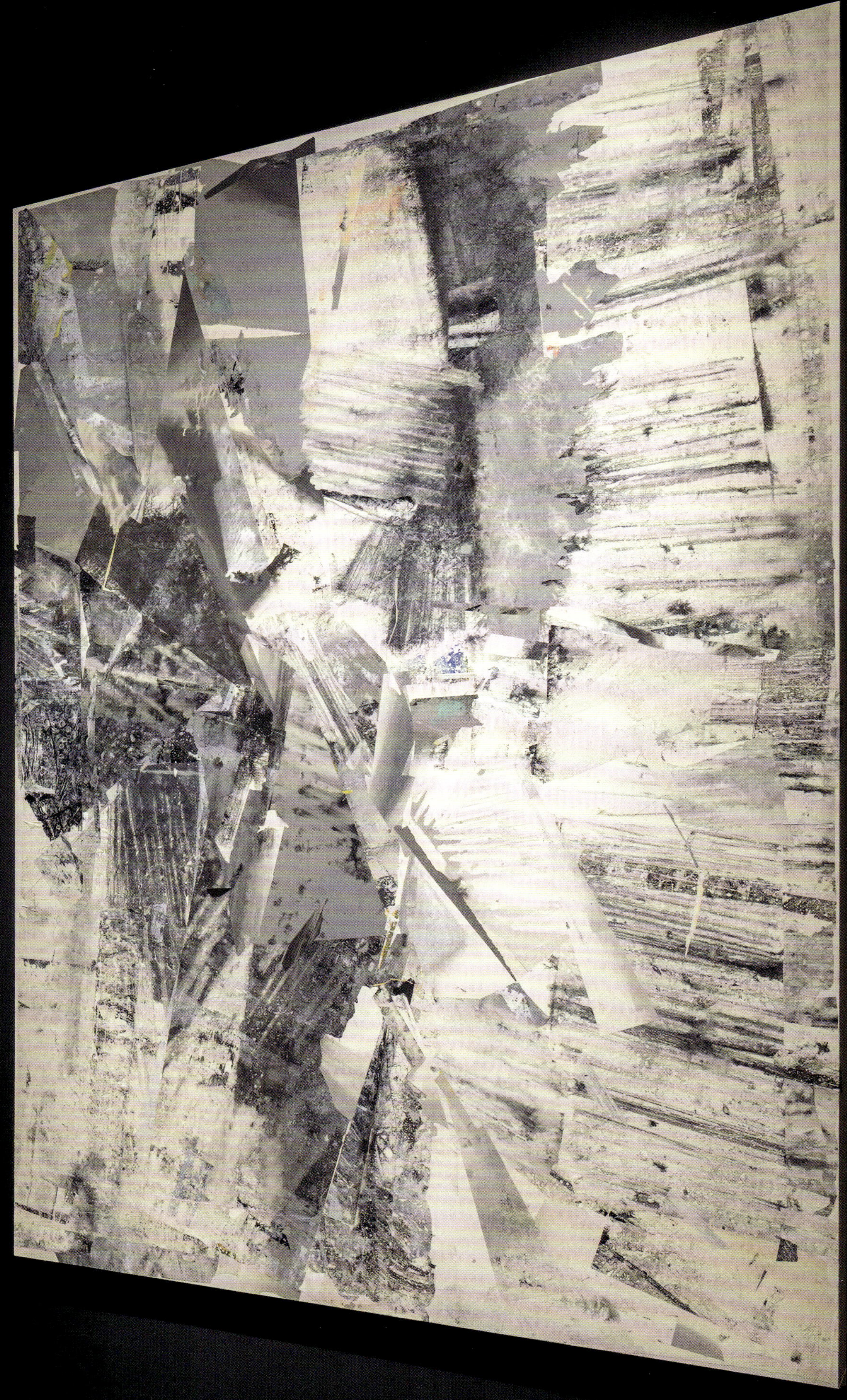

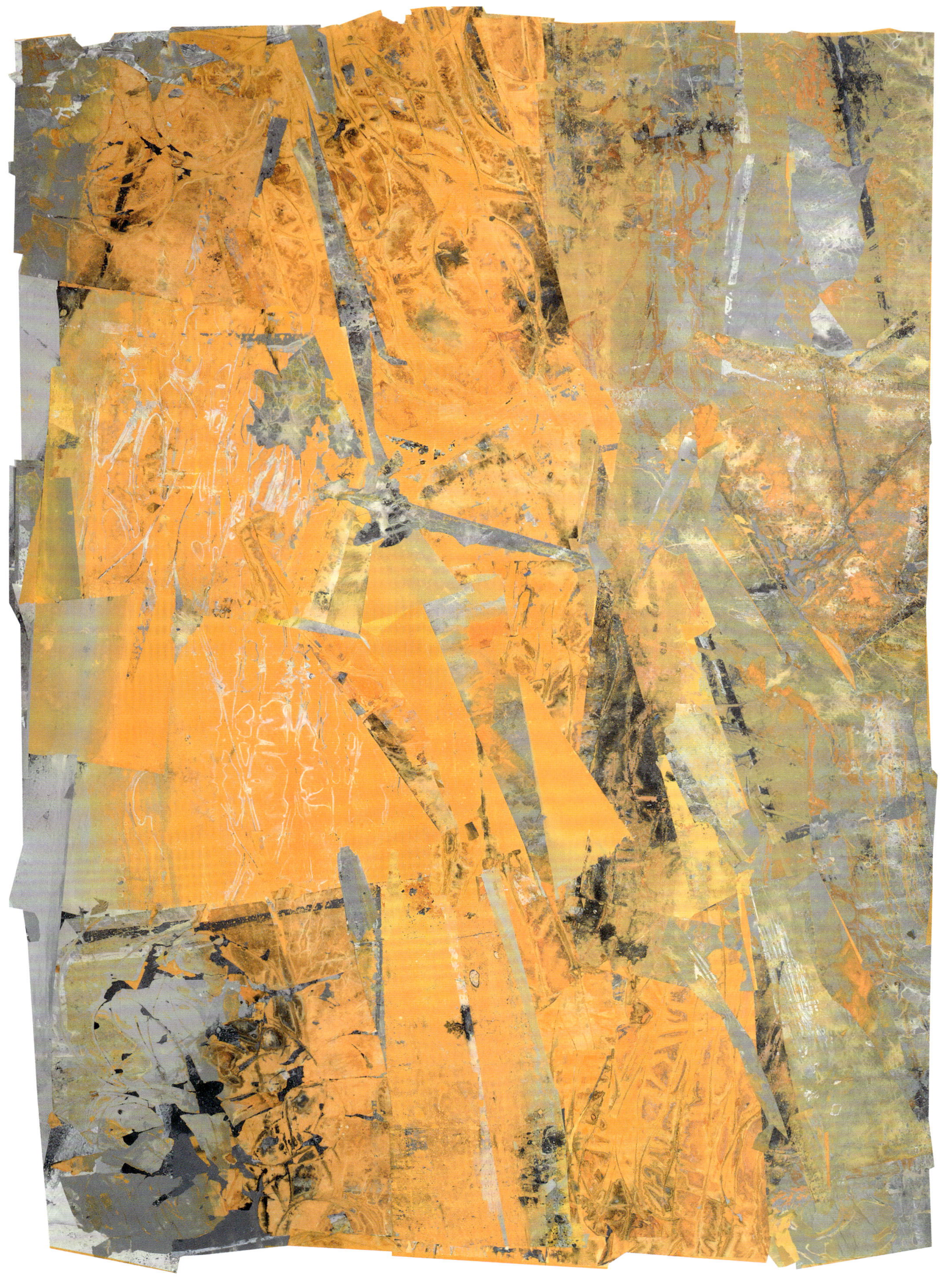

Golden State, 2024
Ink, acrylic, and mineral pigments on xuan paper
155¾ × 109¼ in.
Collection of the artist

Untitled, 2024
Ink, acrylic, and mineral pigments on xuan paper
146⅛ × 106¼ in.
Collection of the artist

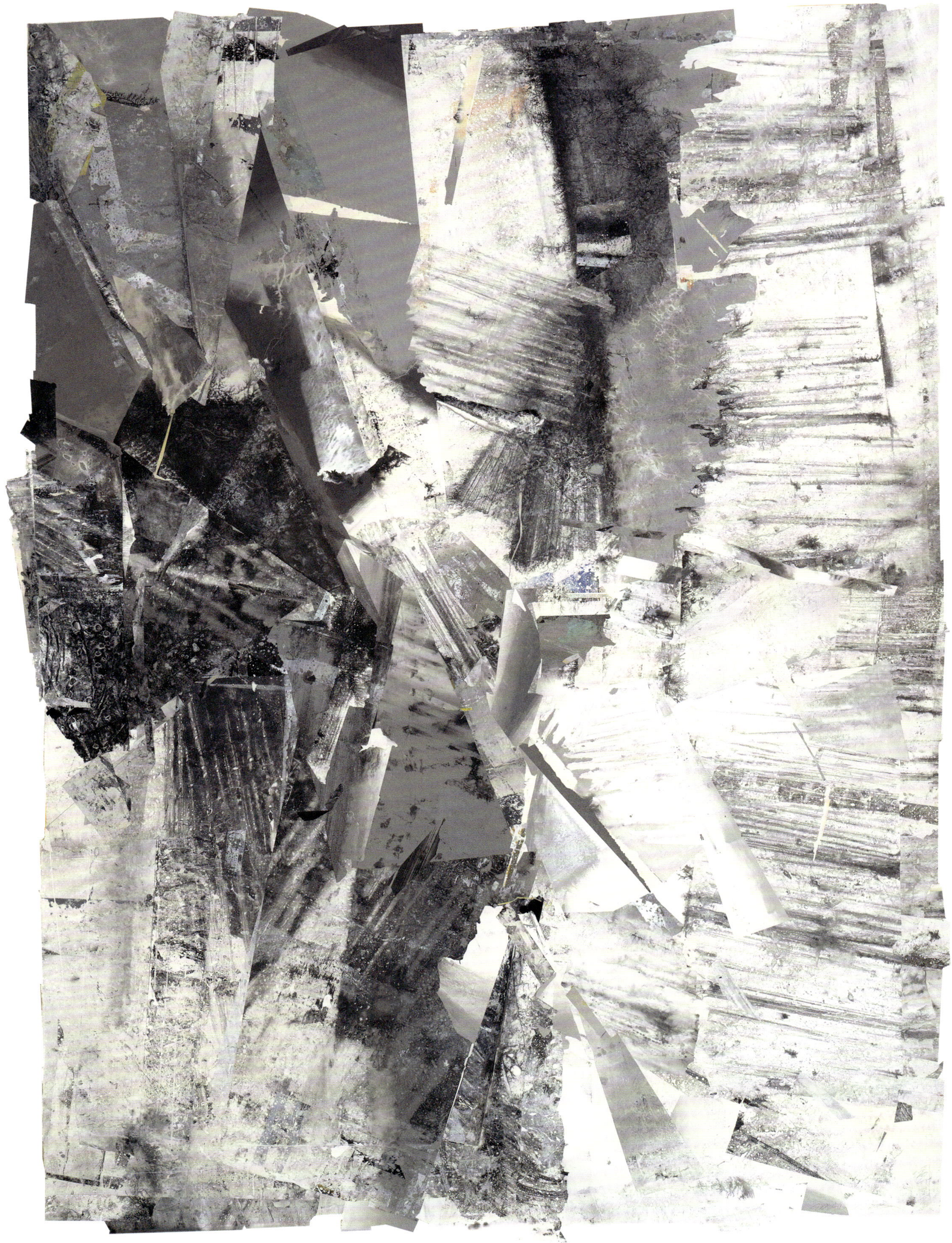

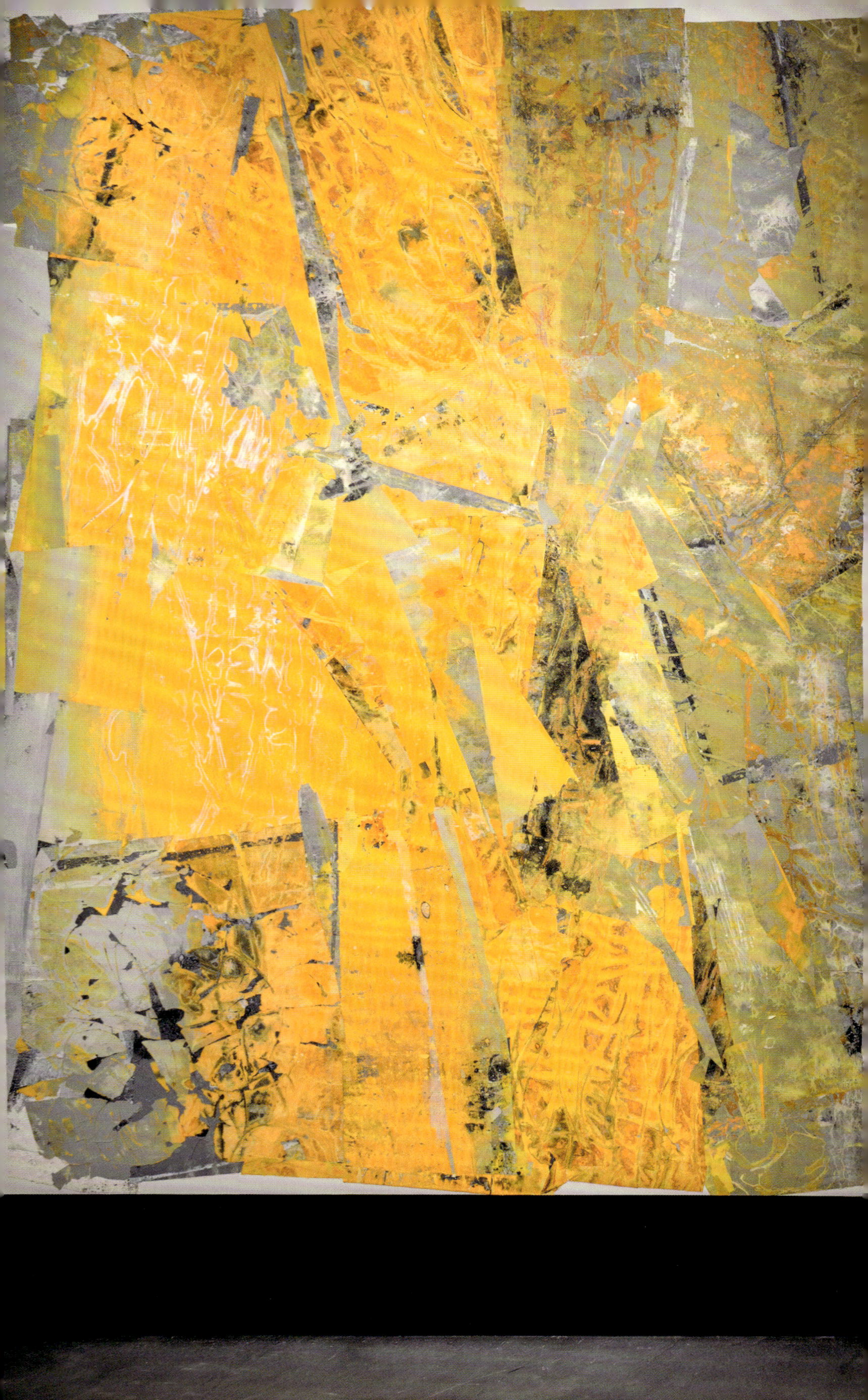

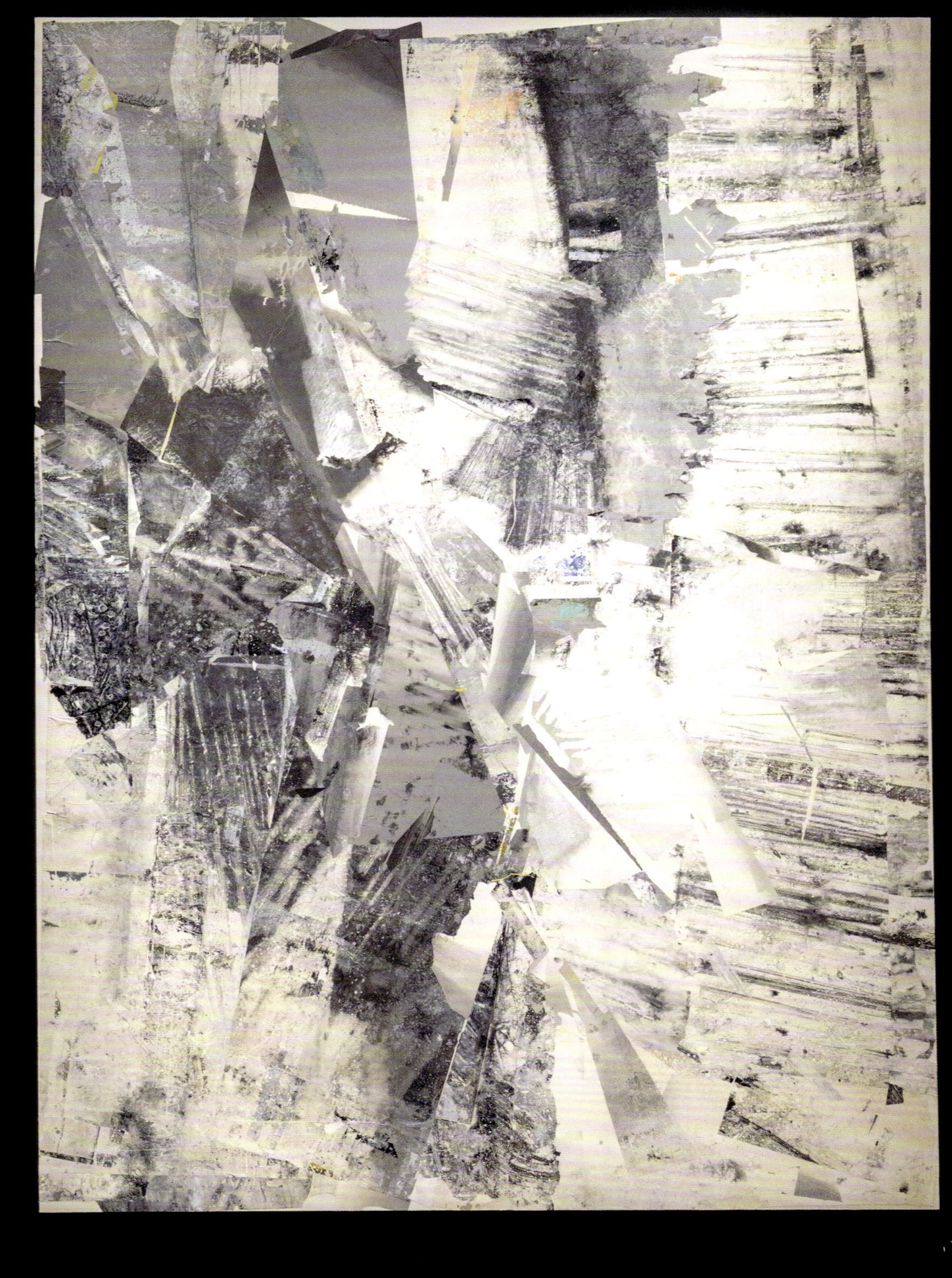

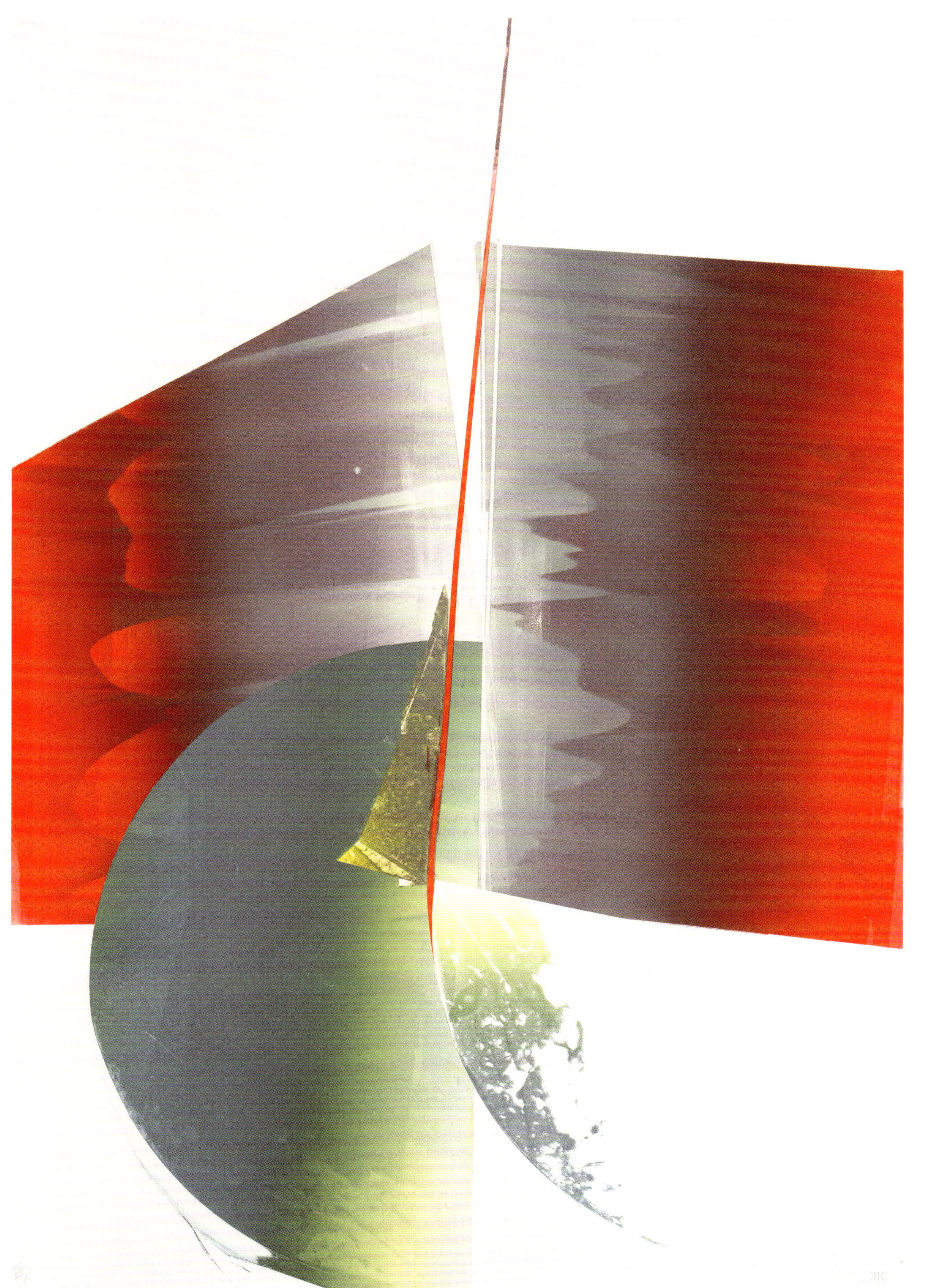

Orbiting Light, 2023
Monotype
42 × 29 in.
Collection of the artist

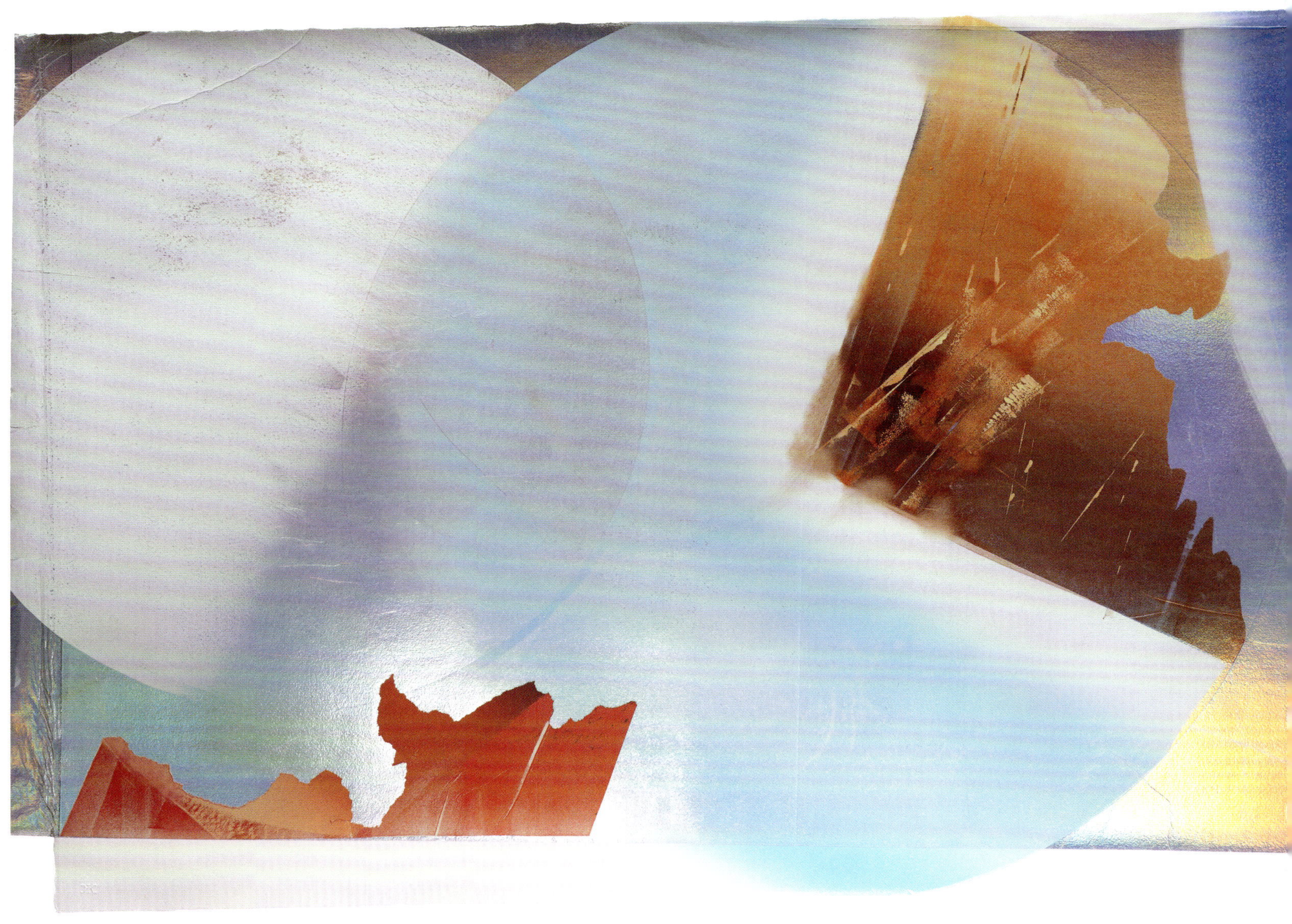

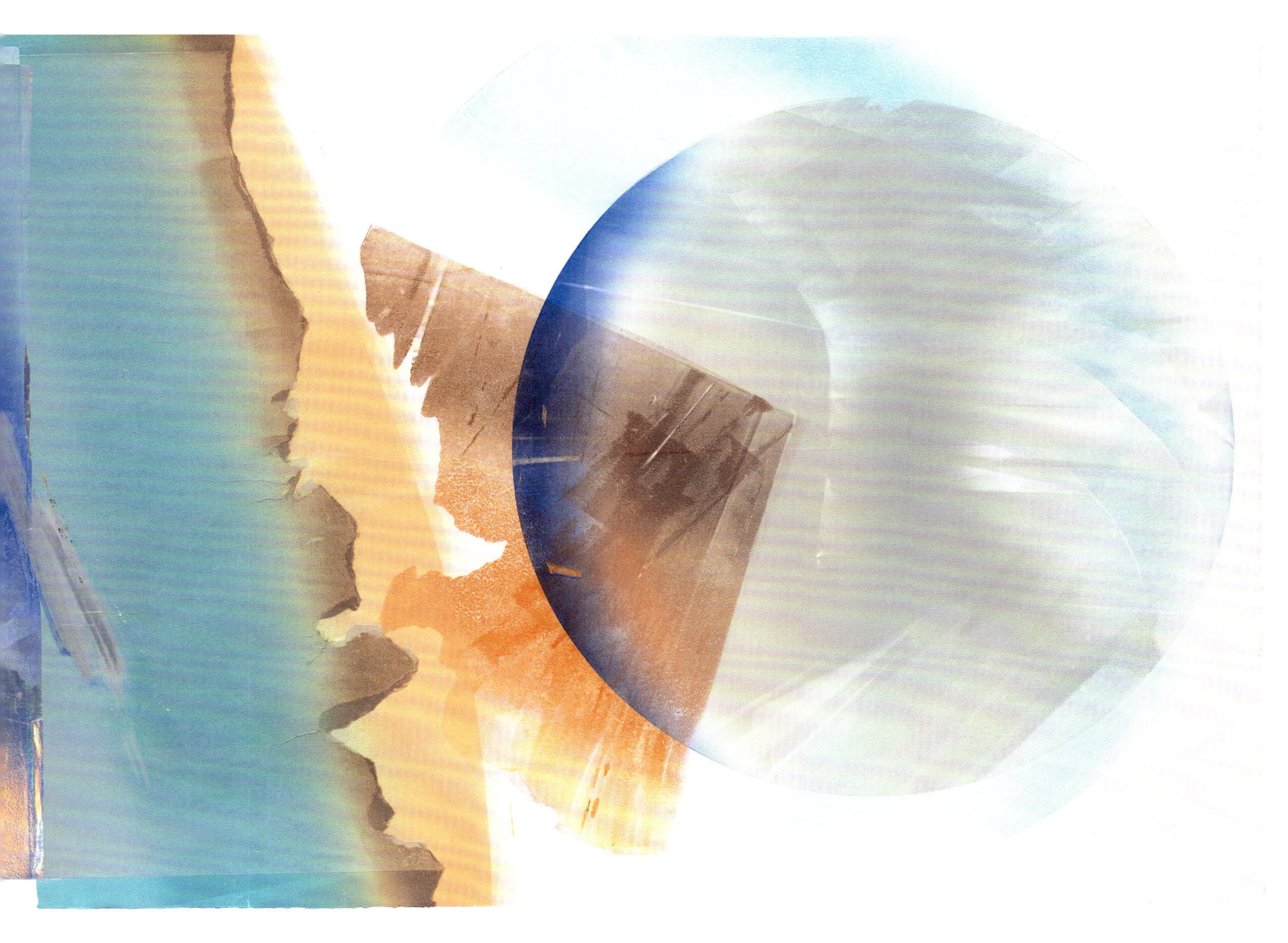

The Poetry of Receding Continents, 2024
Monotype
35 ½ × 92 in.
Collection of the artist

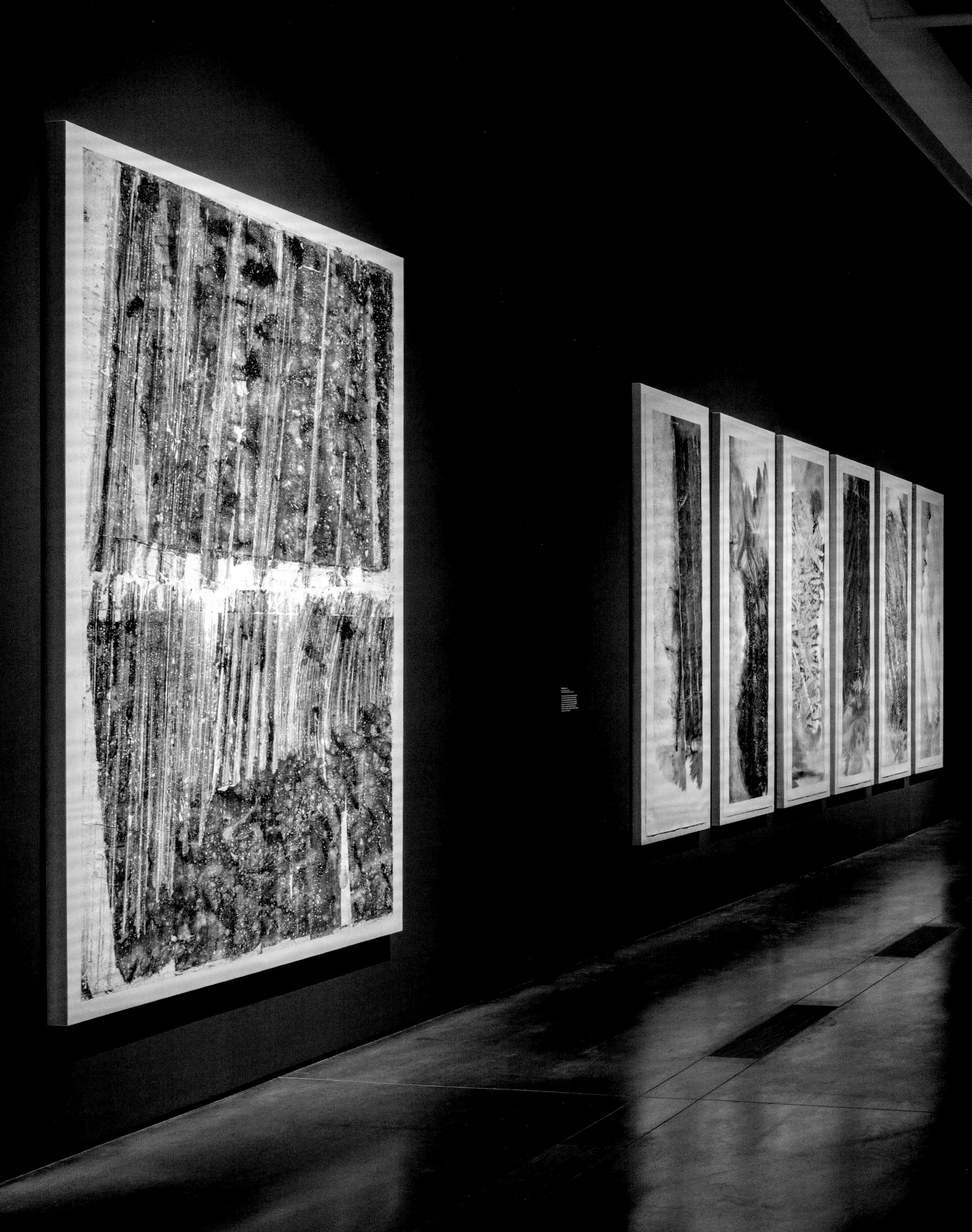

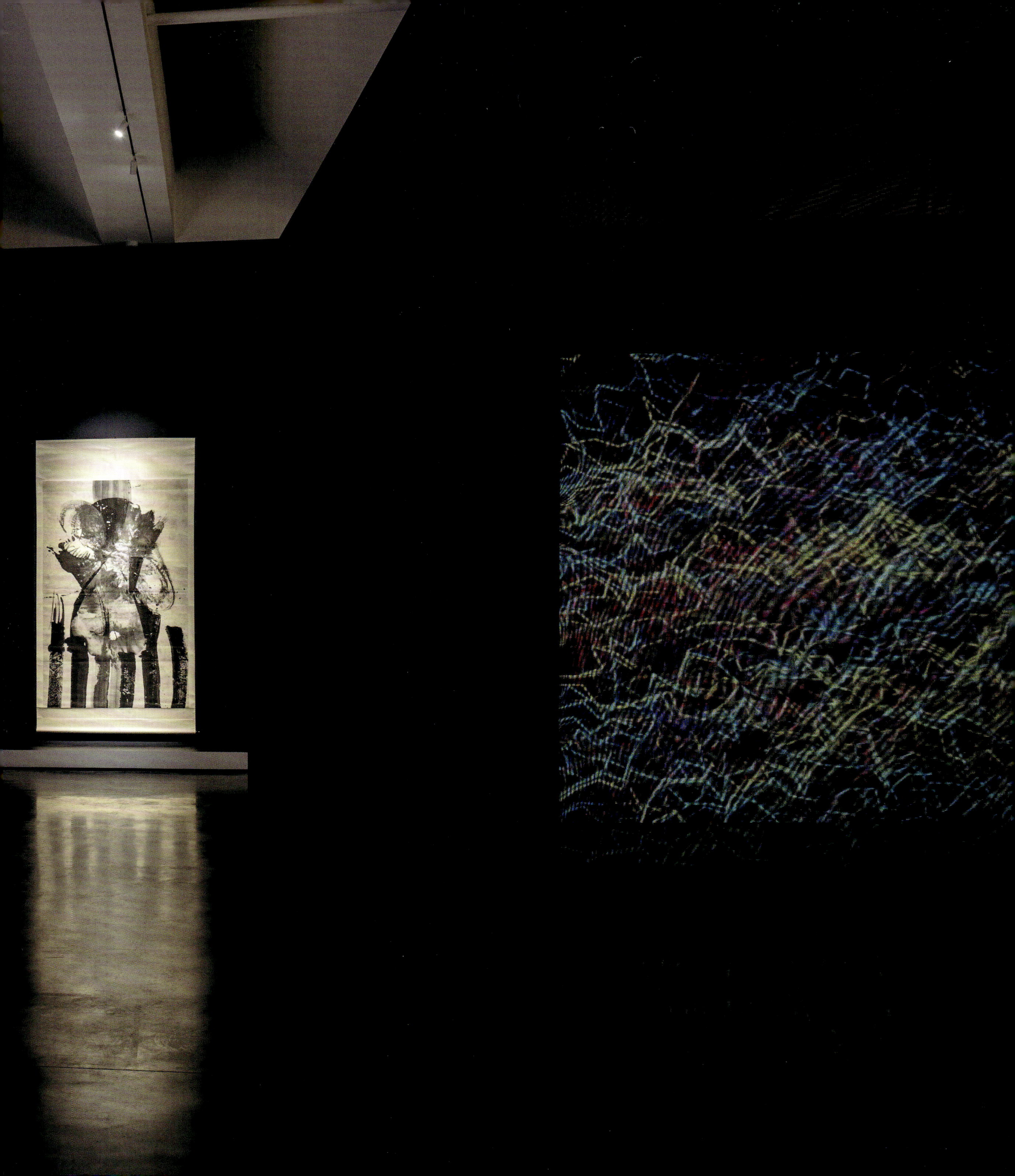

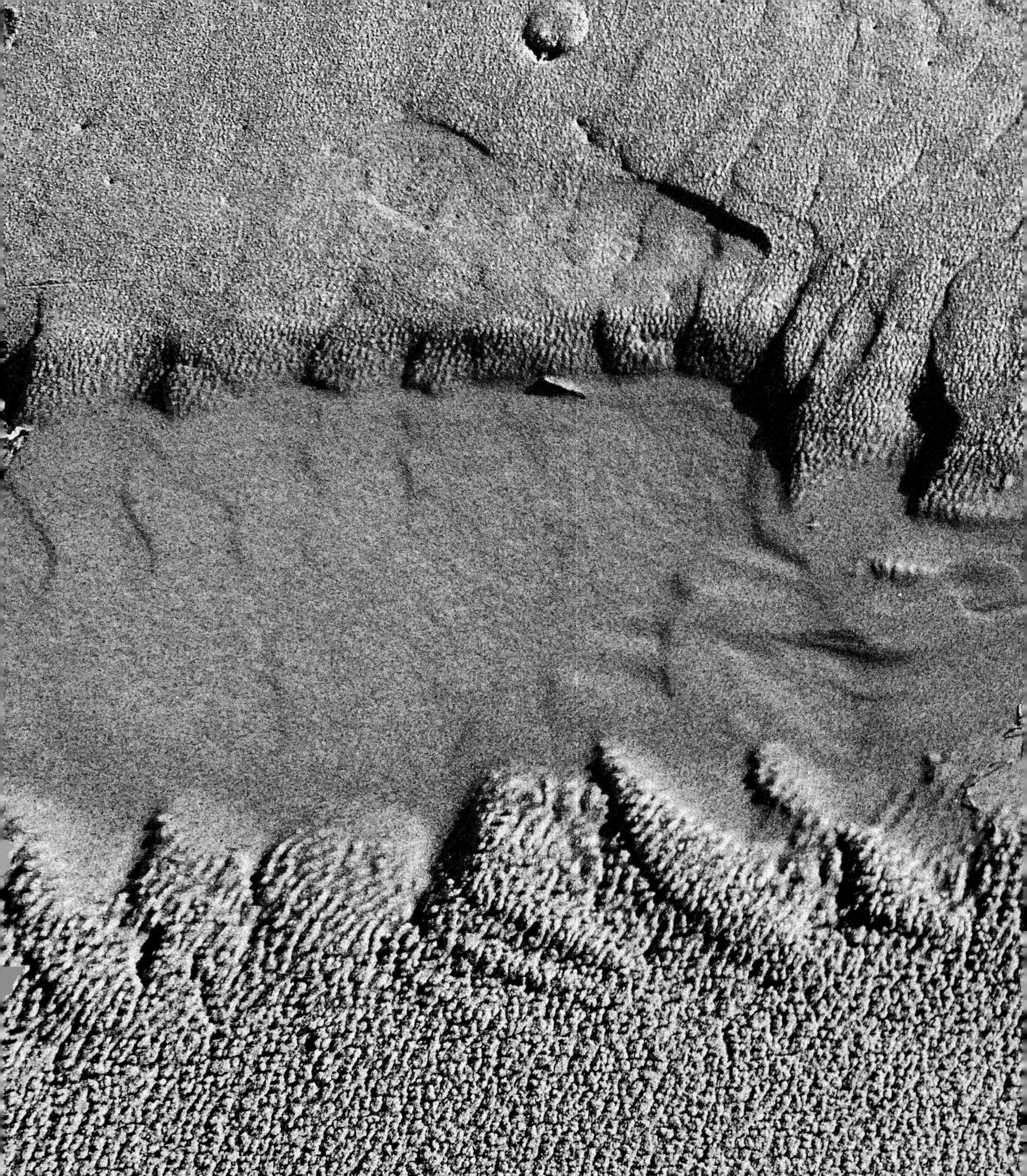

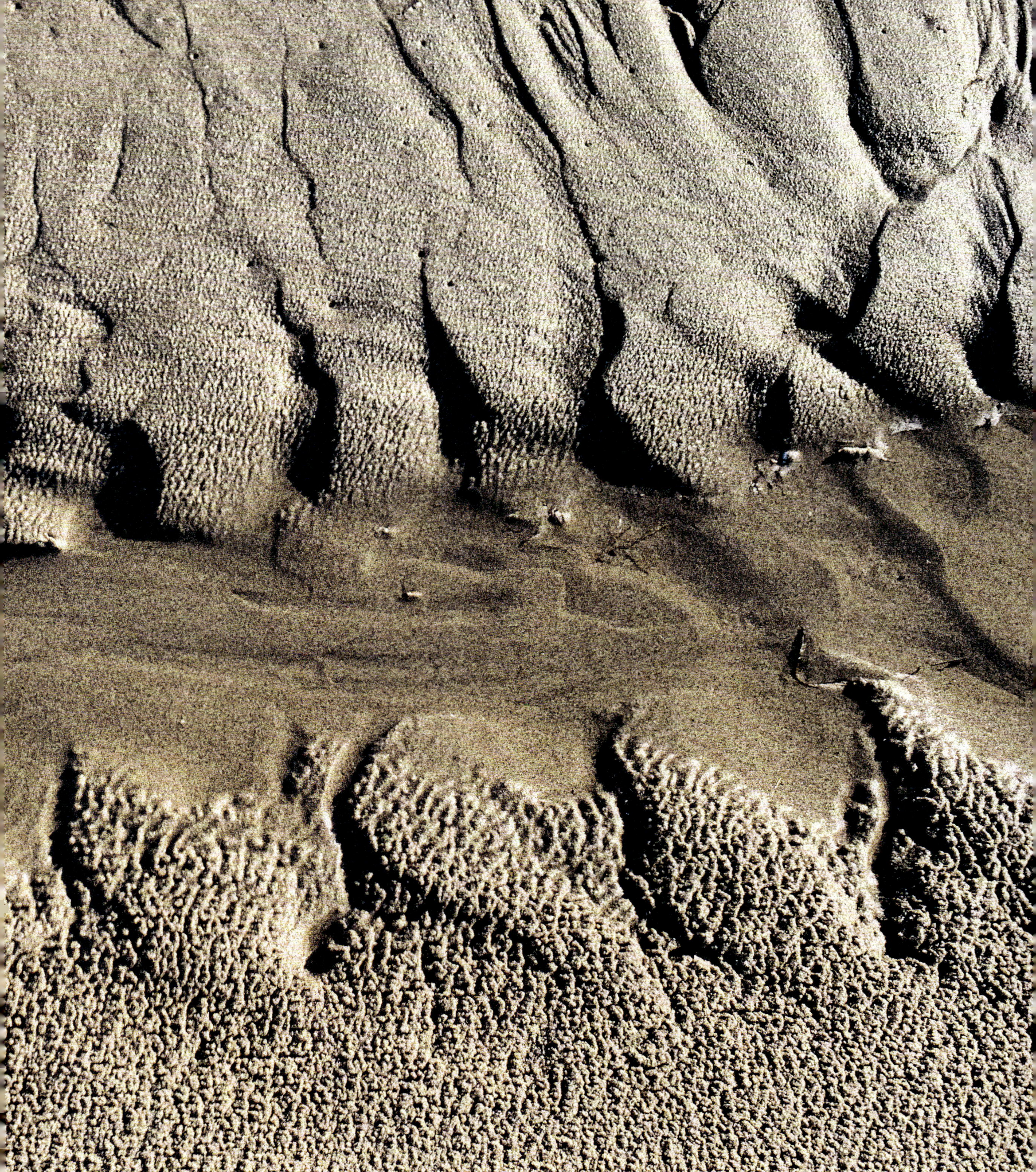

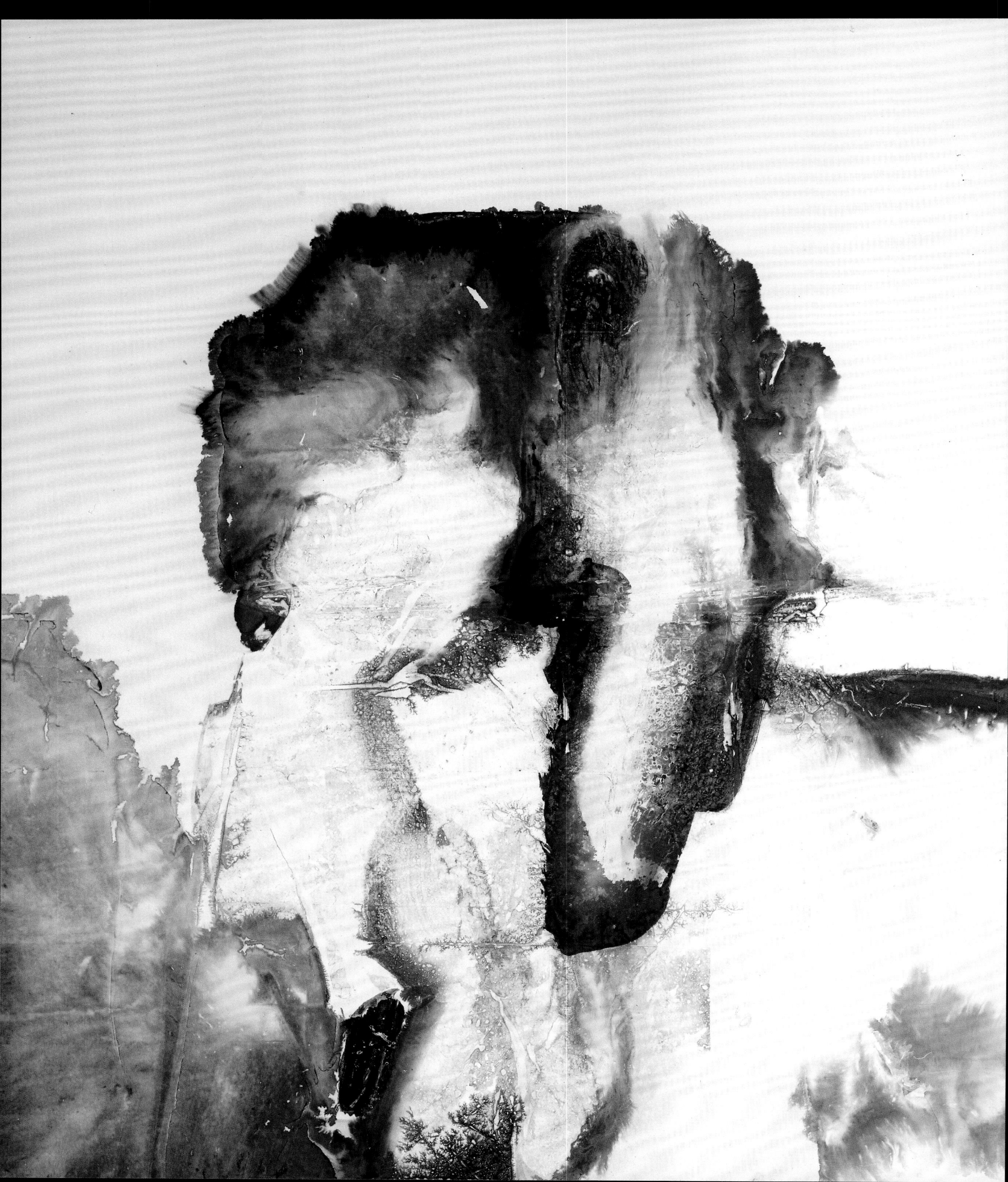

Acknowledgments

To begin, this project would never have become what it is today without the vision and energy of Zheng Chongbin. We have been lucky enough to show Chongbin's work at LACMA on a number of occasions, and each time he has enthusiastically offered his support and insights in the form of workshops, public programs, and guidance. Throughout the planning for this project, we have had countless conversations, emails, reviews, meetings…always inspirational, often surprising, and invariably furthering my understanding of his complex and highly conceptual practice. It has been an honor to curate this exhibition.

I am grateful to our lenders, without whom this exhibition would not be as full and rich with variety: Gérard and Dora Cognié, Akiko Yamazaki and Jerry Yang, and Jennifer and Mark McCormick. My sincere thanks to Stephen Little, Florence & Harry Sloan Curator and Department Head of Chinese & Korean and South & Southeast Asian Art, for his consistent support of my curatorial endeavors at LACMA. I thank Michael Govan, LACMA's CEO and Wallis Annenberg Director, for his enthusiasm over this project and the work of Zheng Chongbin, and for contributing an incisive and stimulating interview to this volume; and Fiona Ragheb, Deputy Director of Curatorial & Exhibitions, for her support of the exhibition.

Many thanks to Celia Yang, Head of Director's Strategic Initiatives, Asia, for her dual roles—finding support for the show and curatorial assisting. Celia, your dedication is beyond admirable. In addition, I am deeply grateful to Nancy Fox, Senior Curatorial Administrator of South & Southeast Asian Art, and Chinese & Korean Art, Vikki Cruz, Exhibitions Coordinator, and Zoe Blackwell, Assistant Registrar, who effortlessly oversaw and managed the exhibition's communications and planning.

Thank you to Craig Yee, for encouraging and supporting the publication of this exhibition catalogue. Thank you, as well, to East West Bank, Fred Gordon, the Li and Zhang Family, Jennifer and Mark McCormick, and the WLS Spencer Foundation for their generous support of this exhibition; Philomena Mariani, editor, for her detailed work; and Susan Chun, Senior Director of Publishing, for guiding the catalogue to completion. Kestrel Rundle, Gina Broze, and Ryan Polich of Marquand Books provided crucial organization (Kestrel and Gina) and thoughtful design (Ryan).

Many people deployed their indispensable skills to bring this exhibition from concept to final installed form. My thanks to Victoria Behner, Associate Director, and Darwin Hu, Art Bridges Fellow, both in Exhibition Design and Production; Julia Latane, Assistant Director of Art Preparation and Installation (API); Matthew Driggs, API Manager, Exhibitions; Mike Held, API Manager of Permanent Collections; Kelsey Lacanilao, API Program Administrator; art preparators Joseph Leavenworth, Daniel Wheeler, David Foster, and Marco Valenzuela; conservators Soko Furuhata, Amanda Burr, and Carinne Klaristenfeld; Christine Ferriter, Gallery Lighting Designer; Jeff Young, Manager of Gallery Construction; and David Armendariz, Mount Maker.

Finally, thank you to my family and community for going to museums with me, encouraging me in the face of imposter syndrome, and being a sounding board for half-baked ideas.

Susanna Ferrell

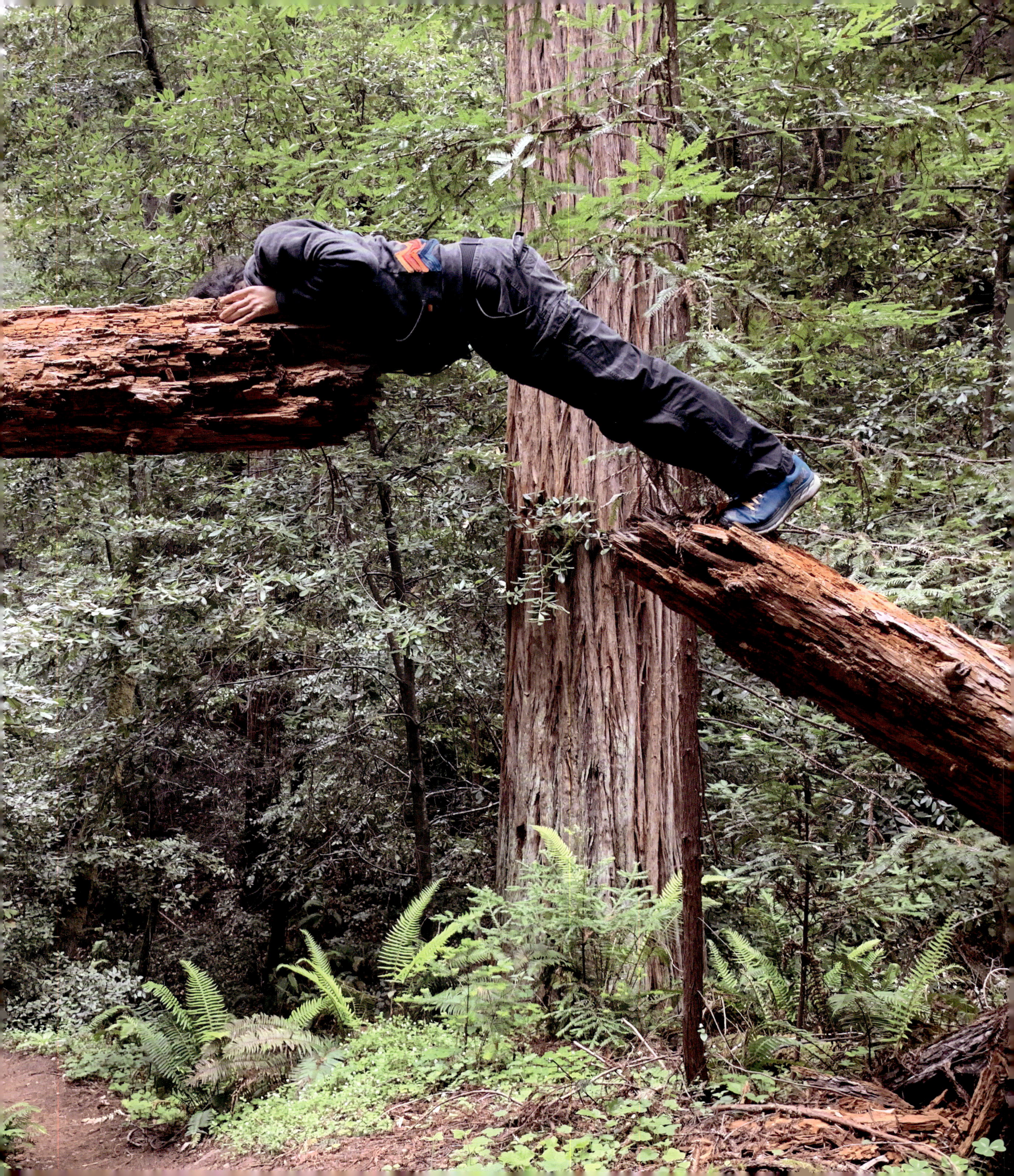

Biography

Zheng Chongbin
Born in 1961, Shanghai
Lives and works in the San Francisco Bay Area

Education

1991
MFA San Francisco Art Institute

1984
BFA Chinese Painting Department, Zhejiang
Academy of Fine Arts (now China Academy of Art),
Hangzhou

Selected Solo Exhibitions

2025
Unfolding, Altman Siegel Gallery, San Francisco

2024
Immeasurable Things, Galerie Du Monde,
Hong Kong

2022
A 10,000 Years View, Hong Kong Museum of Art

2020
I Look for the Sky, Asian Art Museum, San Francisco

2019
Liquid Space, Ryosoku-in Temple, Kennin-ji, Kyoto

2018
Walking Penumbra, INK Studio, Beijing

2017
Zheng Chongbin: Clusters of Memory, Asia
Society, Houston

2016
The Pacific Project: Zheng Chongbin, Orange County Museum of Art, Costa Mesa, California

2013
Zheng Chongbin: Impulse, Matter, Form, INK Studio, Beijing

2011
White Ink: Fresharp Artists' Series, Chinese Culture Center of San Francisco

2010
ZHENG CHONGBIN: Emergent, Valentine Willie Fine Art, Singapore

1988
Chongbin Zheng, Shanghai Art Museum, Shanghai

Selected Group Exhibitions

2023
Summoning Memories: Art Beyond Chinese Traditions, Asia Society, Houston

None Whatsoever, Museum of Fine Art Houston

2021
Ink Dreams: Selections from the Fondation INK Collection, Los Angeles County Museum of Art

2019
Descending from the Above, New Chinese Galleries, Philadelphia Museum of Art

2018
Ink Worlds: Contemporary Chinese Painting from the Collection of Akiko Yamazaki and Jerry Yang, Cantor Arts Center at Stanford University, Stanford, California

2017
The Weight of Lightness: Ink Art at M+, M+ Museum, Hong Kong

Streams and Mountains without End: Landscape Traditions of China, The Metropolitan Museum of Art, New York

2016
Why Not Ask Again, 11th Shanghai Biennale, Power Station of Art

2014
Rendering the Future: Chinese Contemporary Ink Painting Exhibition, Asia Art Center, Beijing

2010
Shanghai: Art of the City, Asian Art Museum, San Francisco

2009
Caligraffiti: Writing in Contemporary Chinese and Latino Art, Pacific Asia Museum, Pasadena

2007
Reboot: The Third Chengdu Biennale, Chengdu, China

1996
Rice / Snails / Pigeons, Meridian Gallery,
San Francisco

1993
Group Six Show, Belcher Studios Gallery,
San Francisco

1985
National Young Artists Exhibition, National Art
Museum of China, Beijing

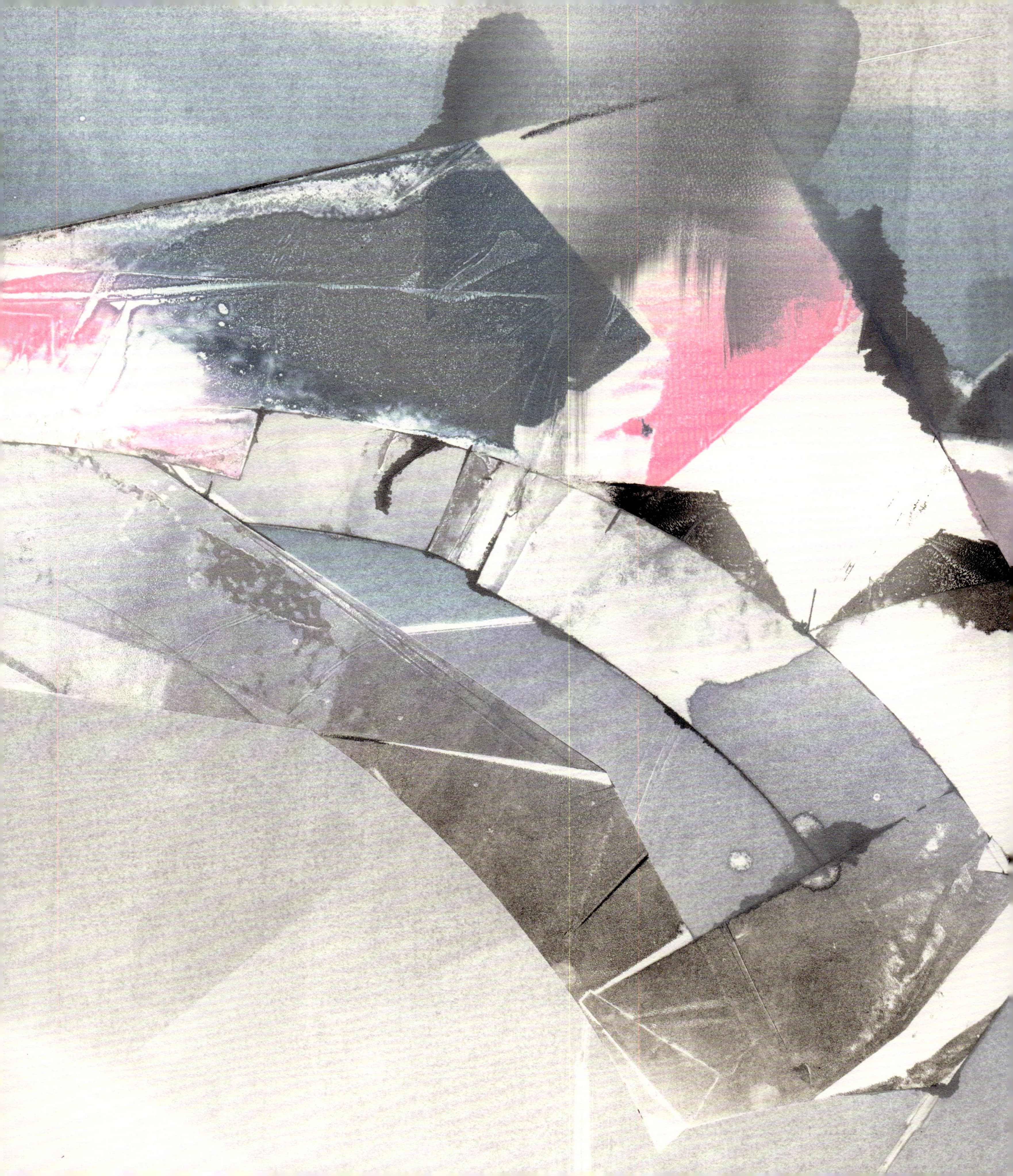

Contributors

Michael Govan is CEO and Wallis Annenberg Director at the Los Angeles County Museum of Art.

Susanna Ferrell is Wynn Resorts Associate Curator of Chinese Art at the Los Angeles County Museum of Art, with a focus on contemporary art of the greater Sinosphere.

Celia Yang is Director of Principal Gifts and Head of Director's Strategic Initiatives, Asia, at the Los Angeles County Museum of Art.

This book is published on the occasion of the exhibition *Zheng Chongbin: Golden State* presented at the Los Angeles County Museum of Art from March 23, 2025, to January 4, 2026.

Published in 2025 by the Los Angeles County Museum of Art, INK Institute, and DelMonico Books • D.A.P.

Los Angeles County Museum of Art
5905 Wilshire Boulevard
Los Angeles, CA 90036
lacma.org

DelMonico Books
available through ARTBOOK | D.A.P.
75 Broad Street, Suite 630
New York, NY 10004
artbook.com
delmonicobooks.com

ISBN: 978-1-63681-182-6
Library of Congress Control Number:
    2025934519

Funding was provided by The WLS Spencer Foundation.

Produced by Marquand Books, Seattle
    marquandbooks.com
Edited by Philomena Mariani
Designed by Ryan Polich
Typeset in Resolve Sans and
    Georgia Pro by Maggie Lee
Proofread by Brynn Warriner
Color management by I/O Color,
    Seattle
Printed and bound in Italy by
    Graphicom

Photography Credits
The following images are those for which additional credits are due. Unless otherwise noted, all photos are © 2025 Zheng Chongbin.

Cover (detail), p. 76: photo by Zhang Hong
pp. 2 (detail), 21 (detail): photo by Nick Lynch
pp. 4 (detail), 58, 60, 61, 72, 94 (detail): photo by Maurice Aeschimann, courtesy of the Fondation INK Collection
pp. 6 (detail), 38 (detail), 39 (detail), 40 (detail), 46 (detail), 47 (detail), 76, 79: photo by Zhang Hong
pp. 10 (detail), 71, 82, 85, 86, 88, 89, 102 (detail): photo by The Image Flow
pp. 13, 17, 19 (detail), 24 (detail), 25 (detail), 29, 30, 92 (detail), 93 (detail): photo by Zheng Chongbin
p. 14: photo by Alan Yeung, courtesy of Ink Studio
p. 15: image by Moodie Younis, courtesy of Zheng Chongbin
p. 18: photo by Jonathan Leijonhufvud, courtesy of Ink Studio
pp. 8, 9, 26 (detail), 48, 49, 54, 56, 57, 63, 66, 67, 74, 75, 80, 81, 90, 91: photo © 2025 Museum Associates/LACMA
p. 28: top photo by Peter Schälchli, Zurich, © 2025 Cy Twombly Foundation
p. 28: bottom photo © 2025 Mark Brest van Kempen
p. 31: courtesy of Zheng Chongbin and Altman Siegel, San Francisco
p. 32: bottom photo © The Cultural Relics Publishing House, Beijing
p. 33: courtesy of Ink Studio
p. 35: Photograph by Warren Silverman, © Whitney Museum of American Art / Licensed by Scala / Art Resource, NY, © 2025 Robert Irwin / Artists Rights Society (ARS), New York
pp. 36, 98 (detail): photo by Peter Sapienza
p. 42: photo by Myriam Thyes
p. 44: courtesy of Gallery 149
pp. 68, 69: photo by Kaz Tsuruta

Cover: Zheng Chongbin, *Golden State*, 2024 (detail)
p. 2: Zheng Chongbin working on *Golden State* in his studio, 2024 (detail)
p. 4: Zheng Chongbin, *Untitled Nº 2*, 1988 (detail)
p. 6: Zheng Chongbin, *Untitled*, 2024 (detail)
pp. 24, 25: Bolinas Beach, Bolinas, California, 2021 (detail).
p. 26: Zheng Chongbin, *Turbulence*, 2014 (detail)
pp. 38, 39: Zheng Chongbin, *Golden State*, 2024 (detail)
p. 40: Zheng Chongbin, *The Poetry of Receding Continents*, 2024 (detail)
pp. 46, 47: Zheng Chongbin, *Untitled*, 2024 (detail)
pp. 92, 93: Limantour Beach, Point Reyes National Seashore, California, 2021 (detail).
p. 94: Zheng Chongbin, *Untitled Nº 9*, 2007 (detail)